Pursuing Excellence in Ministry

Daniel V. Biles

An Alban Institute Publication

The Publications Program of The Alban Institute is assisted by a grant from Trinity Church, New York City.

Library of Congress Catalog Card Number 88-70760
ISBN #1-56699-026-2

TABLE OF CONTENTS

This is a book about excellence in ministry, some of the people who pursue it, and what it takes to do it. This is not another "how-to" manual on the practice of parish ministry. It is an attempt to integrate theological perspectives with actual comments and examples from pastors and laypersons whose churches are noted for their vitality in ministry. At a time when so many in the church are despairing and disparaging of the life and future of congregations, I hope to lift up examples of excellence in ministry among pastors and their congregations.

One basic conviction underlies this book—that the local parish ministry is the heart and soul of the church's life, the place where its ministry of the Gospel is most visibly and effectively carried out. In the words of one pastor I spoke with while doing research for this project, "Parish ministry is simply the most important work in the world to do." To pastors and parishioners whose passion for such ministry has waned in recent years, to parishes that have drifted into passivity or anxious groping for the secret to statistical success, to church hierarchies whose focus has shifted away from the primacy of the parish to staff activities which often get in the way of effective parish work, this book is addressed. My hope and prayer is that the insights here will help the local church once again center itself as the concrete manifestation of the Body of Christ in a given community. Basic things must occur in a parish in order for it to grow in its ministry (in depth as well in as members). By holding up examples of those pastors and parishioners in all sizes of congregations who excel in ministry, I hope to inspire others to think and do what is excellent and worthy of praise (Phil. 4:8).

This book is unapologetically Lutheran in its scope of congregational study and theological perspective, for several reasons. First, the project was originally designed to speak to issues in Lutheranism in America, which over the last several decades has failed to live up to its label as the "sleeping giant" of American Christianity which some were claiming a generation ago.[1] This book was written during a time when three Lutheran bodies were merging to form the new Evangelical Lutheran Church in America, and thus was designed in the hope of providing a focus in mission for the new church for the renewal of its parishes. Second, one of the criteria of excellence in ministry listed in the first chapter is fidelity to the confessional tradition of one's church. For Lutheranism this founding document is the Augsburg Confession of 1530. The central research question, then, sought to discover what was happening in congregations which were noted for their ongoing vitality in their life together while seeking to be faithful to Lutheranism's understanding of the mission of the church. Last, the Lutheran Church is the church with which I am most familiar, and over the years I have been privileged to know many fine congregations and their pastors. This book was written that their excellence in ministry might not be forgotten, but held up for others to see and emulate in their own way in their own situation.

Given this Lutheran focus, though, there is much non-Lutheran readers can gain from this book. They will have to ask if their parish is exercising the ministry in faithfulness to their confessional tradition's understanding of what the church is called to be and do. Inasmuch as the Augsburg Confession proposes to the whole church what ought to be its normative doctrine, Lutheranism's theological vision is for the ecumenical church. The theological perspective of this book, then, should at least spur non-Lutheran readers to define more precisely their understanding of the church and its mission. Finally, on a very down-to-earth, practical level, I am certain that non-Lutheran readers will find that what makes for good parish ministry in Lutheran congregations holds true across the ecumenical church as well.

This project had its origins in Tom Peters' writings on excellence in secular organizations. Sometimes the best insights on the church's life come from the outside in very unintentional ways. Such was the case with Peters' observations concerning what distinguishes good organizations and their leaders from those who perform poorly. Organizations, including the church, can learn much from his writings and tapes about what to do and not to do to be effective.

Peters' first book, *In Search of Excellence,* was a study of America's best-run companies and what contributed to their continued viability in the marketplace. After listening to him, I decided that a similar study ought to be done in the church. So I began to do research—for my education, the edification of my churches and the church, and for fun (with the encouragement of my wife Barbara, who always said I ought to write a book). I must thank, too, the Tom Peters Group in Palo Alto, California, for their great help in getting me started. They shared with me how Peters had conducted his original research, sent me a number of tapes, pamphlets, and articles, *gratis,* and invited me to hear Peters in person in Baltimore in October of 1986. For their continued interest in this project, I am deeply grateful. They are truly an excellent group of people.

The method of research and selection of churches is discussed in the first chapter. Because the project was thoroughly self-designed and financed, certain limitations of time and money prevented me from doing everything I would have liked with this project. Ideally, I would have preferred to spend a weekend in every church I studied, interviewing the pastor and parishioners in depth, observing its environment, and participating in its worship. Unfortunately, I could not afford this financially or in time away from my parish responsibilities. As it was, I was very fortunate to see in person almost every church and pastor except those in Texas. Perhaps in the future another person will pick up some of the loose ends in this book, interviewing more laypersons and going into further detail than I was able to do.

I'm indebted to a number of people who have helped with this project since its inception in June of 1986. First, my thanks to the many pastors and laypersons quoted in these pages who gave their time to respond in writing, by interview, or both. I pray that what I have written is deserving of the time they gave me and the observations they shared. Their names are listed in the Appendix.

The following bishops of the former American Lutheran Church (ALC) and Lutheran Church in America (LCA) were very helpful in recommending pastors and congregations for me to visit: Bishop Howard McCarney, Central Pennsylvania Synod—LCA; Bishop Larry Hand of the Southeast Pennsylvania Synod—LCA; Bishop Ray Heine, Michigan Synod—LCA; and Bishop August Wenzel, my campus pastor while in college, Southern District—ALC.

Along the way a number of people were helpful in giving references, suggestions, or comments: Pastor John Braughler of First Lutheran Church, Pittsburgh, and my sister's father-in-law; Pastor Bill Elbert, who was a neighboring pastor to my congregation in Clifton Heights, Pennsylvania; and Pastor Gordon Simmons of Reformation Lutheran Church, Philadelphia. Pastor Ed Saling, a colleague and good friend from my years at St. Mark's Temple, also provided several good names of pastors to contact. Several friends from college days at Texas Lutheran College gave references or constructive comments: Pastor Chris Matthy, now in Secane, Pennsylvania; Mrs. Lael Cordes-Pitts, Midland, Texas; Mrs. Patricia (Bronstad) Mayes, Troy,

Michigan; and Pastor Tommy Sparks, San Antonio, Texas. My wife's brother-in-law, Cary Richert, was responsible for the very good luck of finding out about Pastor Richard Bieber's ministry in Detroit.

Several laypersons from my parish met with me and offered helpful suggestions: Dave Houck, Paul Pitzer, Harold and Barbara Garretson, and Kay Keller. My thanks also to the Joint Council of the parishes I serve for their openness to and support of this project. I am also indebted to the many fine people I have known and served as intern pastor at Good Shepherd, Cincinnati; St. Mark's-Temple Lutheran Church, Clifton Heights, Pennsylvania; and the current churches I serve in the Bendersville Lutheran Parish.

I thank my parents, Helen and Daniel Biles of York Springs, Pennsylvania, for their assistance and participation in this work and, above all, for being faithful to their vows at my baptism to raise me in the faith that I now am called to preach and teach as a pastor in the church. My father especially was helpful in reading and critiquing portions of the book and in advising me on purchasing the proper computer equipment which made writing this book much easier than would have been possible without it.

Three pastors deserve special mention for their help and participation in this work: Dr. Eric Gritsch, professor of Church History at the Lutheran Theological Seminary at Gettysburg and one of the foremost scholars on Martin Luther today, read the first draft of this book and offered helpful suggestions and resources for certain sections.

My good friend of many years and role model in ministry, Pastor John Cochran of Philadelphia, was with me from the start of this project with names and insightful observations. He also reviewed the first draft. I have often said that "pound-for-pound" John Cochran is the best pastor I've ever met.

My intern pastor, oftentimes still mentor, and good friend, Peter Rudowski, probably shaped this study through his suggestions and observations more than any other pastor with whom I talked. My special thanks to him for a Memorial Day weekend together in 1987, during which he did a page-by-page critique which was most helpful. I don't know any pastor who is more insightful on the dynamics of parish life, nor listens harder and more respectfully to the suggestions, concerns, and ideas of his parishioners so as to use their talents in the church's ministry.

And most of all, I thank my wife, Barbara, for her strong support and encouragement and for going along with the sacrifice it took to accomplish this task. Speaking of excellence, I'm reminded of Proverbs 31:29 (RSV): "Many women have done excellently, but you surpass them all."

CHAPTER I

Searching for Excellence

"I don't know why they send pastors right out of seminary to dying churches."

"All we pastors and congregations in this area are trying to do is hold on until the Kingdom comes."

These two inspirational comments welcomed me to the parish ministry in my first year after ordination. Ten years later I still vividly recall those comments, for three reasons: First, the sentiment expressed in them is still very alive and much more widespread than I suspected when I first heard them. Second, I refuse now, as I did then, to accept the pessimism and despair about the vitality of the church's mission embodied in those two remarks. And the last reason is a question: Why, given the joyous Good News of Jesus Christ as Lord and Saviour of all, would committed Christians, both laity and clergy, come to such a pessimistic conclusion about their congregation and its ministry? I am sure that neither of the two people who made the comments above, nor others like them, started out with such a negative attitude about the church and its ministry. So, what brought them to such despair and unbelief?

Taken together, the comments and my reaction to them provided the occasion and the interest to write this book. But, my purpose in writing is not to dwell on the bad news of today, but to focus on the good: Excellence in ministry still abounds in the church in general and the Lutheran Church in particular. Indeed, it flourishes! Despite all the upheavals in society in general, in spite of rapid change in their local environments, there are a lot of congregations out there that have not only managed to survive, but have grown in depth of ministry and, in some cases, in numbers as well. There are pastors out there in all sorts of situations and locations who report they are having fun in the ministry and are excited about the church's mission in the world. This book is about such pastors and their congregations and why they are doing so well while so many other congregations seem to be, in the words of clergy and laity alike, "dying" or "just holding on."

Yes, excellence in ministry still abounds, in spite of the general stagnation in the Lutheran Church for the last generation. Baptized membership in Lutheranism in America has declined for the last twenty years, especially among our youth. The percentage of those who remain in the church after Confirmation has fallen even more dramatically. Members in the Lutheran Church are aging faster than the population at large. Yet, there are parishes—some of which will be named in the chapters to come—who are defying these statistics in their vitality.

More than this, these parishes have done so with an absence of the paranoia afflicting many other congregations. Today laity and pastors grope desperately for solutions to remedy the decline in the Lutheran Church. Paper programs are churned out by staffers in the church hierarchy and applauded as the latest snake-oil cure for our ailments. Forsaking fidelity to Lutheranism's confessional tradition, pastors flock to "how-to" programs for church growth and anxiously discuss what is needed to make the church "relevant" for today. All of a sudden we find "evangelism" occupying the top notch on the bureaucratic agenda (although usually the focus is not on the literal meaning of *euanggelion*—speaking the Gospel—but on its modern-day usage—adding people to the church rolls). The definition of ministry has been stretched to cover almost any activity that goes on in a church. One pastor lamented:

> Our churches have become 'busy' places, full of 'programs,' all working for success, competing against other religious franchises, from aerobics to bingo. This is bull; it reduces the church in the eyes of people, and certainly does not justify sitting on tax-exempt space.

Yet, with all this going on, there are parishes out there which simply seek to carry out the ministry of the Gospel. Theirs is not a quest for success, but for faithfulness, for excellence in doing what God calls the church to do. And—lo and behold!—in doing it they inevitably find that survival takes care of itself. Indeed, many grow numerically as well. These parishes prove the words of one pastor who wrote, "All this Lutheran stuff about Word and Sacraments really works!"[1]

In like manner there are pastors out there excelling in ministry who have not succumbed to the pitfalls afflicting so many other clergy: incidences of chemical dependency, depression, divorce, escaping the demands of parish life for more idyllic settings where they do not have to face the trials and tribulations of the parish, or leaving the ministry altogether. Said one army chaplain to me a few years ago, "The military chaplaincy might be more physically demanding, but at least I don't have to put up with all those nights out at meetings, arguments with Council people and the crap members gave me."

In 1985 Rev. Neal Boese was called to the Michigan Synod of the Lutheran Church in America as Director of Evangelism Emphasis. Seeking to develop programs to meet their needs, he initially visited the pastors of the synod. In the course of his 125 visits, repeatedly and often with great emotion pastors expressed high degrees of frustration, a sense of failure and even despair about their congregations and their ministries. One suspects that similar results would be found in surveys of pastors in other synods. Indeed, one finds that pastors not only despair over their situations, some seem to have despaired over the viability of Lutheranism itself and have sought success for their ministries from other sectors of religious life. It is not uncommon, for example, to hear the virtues of Robert Schuller extolled among Lutheran clergy. Some have even created little "Hour of Power" churches of their own. Even among some church officials there seems to be a lack of confidence in the ministry of Word and Sacrament as the means by which the church is created and sustained. More than once I have heard of officials who discouraged mission pastors from having weekly Communion in their mission churches because, in the words of one, "Weekly Communion would turn people off." Others are caught up in the numbers game. In one synod report the "bottom line" in the church was defined as "net growth in members."

Yet some pastors have not fallen into despair over the viability of the ministry of the Gospel in general or their exercise of it in particular. They stand out as shining lights to others of what can be done, regardless of the situation. They prove excellence in ministry still abounds in the church. What follows is a report of what I found going on in parishes which excel in ministry.

During the last half of 1986 I interviewed pastors and laypeople from nearly four dozen churches in the East, Midwest, and Southwest. The project traces its inspiration to an inauspicious event one evening in late 1985. Having cooked and cleaned up dinner for the family, I quickly scanned the TV listings for the night and, for no particular reason, tuned in a PBS broadcast, "An Evening With Tom Peters," author of the fabulously successful books on American business, *In Search of Excellence* and *A Passion for Excellence*. As I listened to the program, which was a taping of one of his speeches, I thought to myself, "Much of what he is saying here has great rele-

vance to the day-to-day practice of ministry. Pastors and congregations could learn a lot from this." Through reading and listening to
his audiotapes I became more familiar with Peters' observations on
excellence in organizations and began to think, "Someone ought to
do a similar study on what contributes to excellence in ministry."
Which led me to a final conclusion: "Why not do it yourself?" So,
for my own benefit, the education of the members of my churches,
and, through publication, the wider church, I began the research
that has resulted in this book.

As I began the project, it was necessary to clarify my criteria for
excellence in ministry before I could interview pastors and examine
their churches. What are the marks of excellence in ministry in the
parish setting? Two criteria emerged as guidelines for this study.

First and foremost, excellence in ministry has to be marked by
fidelity to the church's confession of faith. This is not a study of successful religious organizations in general. Success is measured first
and foremost by fidelity to what Jesus commands the church to be
and to do. Our Lord makes it clear that not every person (or
church) who piously says, "Lord, Lord," and carries an impressive
portfolio of accomplishments in ministry will be recognized as a
faithful follower at the last day (Matthew 7:21-23). Success in the
faith is measured by fidelity to the faith in which we are baptized
(John 8:31-32; Gal. 5:1; Eph. 4:1; et.al.).

This is why the study was conducted solely among Lutheran congregations and pastors. Not only is it the church with which I am
most familiar and concerned about its vitality, but Lutheranism has
been defined since its inception as a confessional movement within
the Church Catholic. Its founding document, the Augsburg Confession of 1530, was and, properly understood, continues to be a proposal of a group of Christians within the universal church
concerning what ought to be normative doctrine for the Church
Catholic.[2] Thus, the first mark of excellence in ministry for Lutheran
churches has to be fidelity to what the Lutheran Confessions understand the essential work of the church to be. In briefest expression,
this is Word and Sacrament ministry:

> This [The one holy Christian Church] is the assembly of all be-
> lievers among whom the Gospel is preached in its purity and
> the holy sacrament administered according to the Gospel.[3]

This quote from the Augsburg Confession, the prime confessional document of the Lutheran Church, points to a constellation of
basic theological convictions which make for Lutheran identity, what

Lutherans regard as indisputable requisites for the life and work of the church. To delineate further, these would be:

—a focus on the Gospel of justification by faith apart from works (Augsburg Confession, Article IV) as the distinctive message the church bears in the world;

—the divinely instituted office of the ministry, conferred in ordination, of the Word and Sacraments, which are the means of grace through which the Holy Spirit works faith and creates the church for its mission (Augsburg Confession, Article V);

—that the church, created by the Word and Sacraments, is a universal priesthood of all believers which, through the calling and gifts of the Spirit given in baptism, participates in the mission Jesus conferred upon the church through the commands he gave to the apostles (Matthew 28, Acts 1, et.al.);

—the Scriptures as the apostolic authority for what the church preaches and teaches in carrying out its mission, and the 16th-century Lutheran Confessions to safeguard what the church preaches and teaches and how it orders its life.[4]

I cannot understate this concern for confessional fidelity. Lutheranism's obsession in this area is rooted in the confessional nature of the Christian faith before the world (cf. Acts 1:8; Romans 1:16; Phil. 2:11, for example). It is precisely laxity on this point which is working to weaken the church's witness in America today. We have taken a smorgasbord approach to religious commitment in which the confession of faith is jettisoned for whatever suits one's interests and needs for self-expression and fulfillment. A sloppy, sentimental piety assumes all religions are "going to the same place," so why not take a dash of Robert Schuller here, Fundamentalism there, modern Social Gospel here, religious patriotism there? The outgrowth has been a religious goulash fulfilling of the prophecy of 2 Timothy 4:3: "For the time is coming when people will not endure sound teaching, but having itching ears they will accumulate for themselves teachers to suit their own likings." Diluted in the process has been the adherence to the Gospel of justification by faith—"the article on which the church stands or falls," as classical Lutheranism puts it—and, therefore, the church's essential work. Indeed, in viewing American Christianity today, one is driven to ask, "Whatever happened to Galatians 1:8: 'But even if we or an angel from heaven should preach a gospel other than the one we preached to you, let him be eternally condemned'?"

Interestingly enough, my last research interview confirmed this concern for confessional faithfulness which I had decided upon at the start of the project. In a conversation with the Rev. Richard Neuhaus, the topic of evangelism in the local church arose. Neuhaus remarked that two distinct approaches can be observed in the church today. One, opted for by the Church Growth Movement, Robert Schuller and others, makes reaching the unchurched person the focus of everything that is done in the congregation. Everything from worship on down is geared to attracting and holding the unchurched person. What invariably results, he observed, is a "bastardized" Christianity which, though numerically successful, is not what the Lord has commanded the church to be and to do. The other approach, which he tried to implement in his own dynamic ministry at St. John's the Evangelist in Brooklyn, is to nurture the life of the congregation within the church's confessional tradition so that its life together in worship exemplifies what the church is called to be as fully and as vibrantly as possible. In this strengthening and deepening, other people become attracted to the church as a community whose life they want to be a part of. "Evangelism," he commented, "occurs through the church by its being the church." (My own observations on the Church Growth Movement, its positive aspects and its difference from the pursuit of excellence in ministry are contained in the last chapter.)

What is commonly understood as success in statistical terms, then, must occur with fidelity to what Jesus has called the church to be and to do, not at the expense of it. Thus, in beginning to look for congregations to study or in asking people for references, the first criterion was a clear Lutheran identity and commitment to what confessional Lutheranism understands the church to be about. To be sure, the Lord himself makes the final determination on the faithfulness of his followers. But, insofar as the church in general (in the Ecumenical Councils of AD 300-600) and Lutheranism in particular, through its confessional writings, have made decisions of doctrine which describe the nature and work of the church, these criterion were used in selecting pastors and congregations for this study. Of course, these are not the only pastors and churches one could include in this study; but, given the limitations of time and money, they were the most accessible.

The second mark of excellence in ministry has to do with the way a congregation functions in its environment. That is, congregations which do well in their ministry are responsive to the environment in which they minister and the changes which occur there. They exhibit an ongoing vitality in ministry which is the result of consistently attempting to bring the Gospel to bear on the lives of their members and the surrounding community. Faced with changes in their surroundings, they respond by carrying out their work as a church of Jesus Christ in a way that, over time, continues to attract people to the congregation. They are prime examples of what Warren Bennis and Burt Nanus, in their book *Leaders,* call a "learning organization"—an organization which does more than simply learn how to respond to known and recurring problems (maintenance learning), but which exhibit "innovative learning," the capability to respond to new situations and anticipate changes in creative ways which enhance the life of the organization and enable it to accomplish the purposes for which it exists.[5]

Again, numerical size was not a prime determinant here. The above characteristic can and does exist in churches of every size. Of particular interest were those congregations which continued to carry out and develop their ministries in situations where their environment was going through marked transition—for example, churches in areas undergoing racial, ethnic or economic change. The former two are of particular interest in regard to Lutheran churches, which are in many places still tied to their ethnic German and Scandinavian populations. Though the Gospel of Jesus Christ is universal in perspective, many Lutheran congregations in areas where they have lost their traditional ethnic constituencies have closed their doors. Yet, not all have. It is a mark of their excellence in ministry—indeed, their faithful witness to the Gospel's universal character—that they not only survive the population changes, but in some cases thrive numerically as well. Not overlooking the work of the Holy Spirit, what is it about these churches that makes them different from those who fail to adapt to the same changes?

With these two criteria in mind, I began my research by seeking pastors and congregations to study. Some, of course, I knew first hand from my years in the ministry. Others came from a variety of sources, which I mention in the Preface. At times the project seemed to assume a life of its own and contact opportunities would arise "by grace." A case in point: On a trip to Michigan to see some pastors, my brother-in-law, a lay professional in the Lutheran Church-Missouri Synod, mentioned my project to a colleague of his, who in turn referred an excellent contact to me in Pastor Richard Bieber of Detroit, who in turn arranged for me to meet another superb reference, Rev. Neal Boese of the Michigan Synod. Except for those from Texas and one from Iowa, all interviews were done in person. In the case of the former, as with many of the latter, a questionnaire profiling the congregations was completed.

What was unique about these pastors and their churches? Again, in spite of the changes occurring in their parishes, their local envi-

ronment, and the society as a whole, these churches have adapted
and grown in their ministry of the Gospel. Some have grown numerically as a result, some have not. All are regarded by others as
highly creative and dynamic ministries that are distinctly, though not
in every jot and tittle, faithful to the Lutheran tradition.

The Results: An Overview

Myriads of books, most notably by Lyle Schaller, have been written
in recent years on parish management, church administration and
program development. Any Christian bookstore is loaded with
"how-to" manuals on the church, from finances to the Sunday
School to fund-raising to doing the planning of worship to strategies for growth. The sheer volume of materials is exhausting to ab-
sorb, let alone put into actual practice. The danger in all this is that,
like so many other areas of life, the practice of ministry is reduced
to a series of techniques which are applied to congregations to produce certain desired results.

This book is not a "how-to manual." It is not a collection of
"bright ideas" to be taken and tried out on a congregation. In fact,
the results of this study suggest that, for all that has been written on
"how to run a parish," key elements are present in any congregation, any pastor, which is doing excellent ministry—even taking into
account different styles of pastoral leadership and practice, and varying congregational organization and programs. The list of pastors
and churches (see Appendix) varied in every conceivable way, yet
key themes emerged again and again. In fact, as pastors and laity
talked about what makes for excellence in parish ministry, exact
words, phrases, and sentences were repeatedly used to describe
what was taking place in their parishes.These common principles
mentioned in most of the parishes are the *foundations* and the
expressions of excellence in ministry.

The Foundations of Excellence

MISSION: To paraphrase a phrase from Tevye the Milkman in "Fid-
dler on the Roof," mission is knowing who you are and what God
expects you to do. Good pastors and congregations have this self-
awareness. It is a clear and commonly-held understanding of what
ministry is and how it is to be carried out in a given parish. It is
why, as one pastor mentioned, "how-to" programs do not work. If a
parish does not know what it exists to be and do, no amount of
"busyness" and "quick-fix" ideas will substitute.

LEADERSHIP: The creation and articulation of, the focusing attention on, and the developing commitment to a vision of what God is calling the congregation to be and to do—and the concrete form its mission in the community should take—marks the excellent parishes. Such leadership is primarily and indispensably exercised by the pastor(s). It is rooted in the pastor's self-awareness of being called by God to exercise the office of ministry and refined by training in the various disciplines and tasks of pastoral ministry. It is exercised through an ordained minister's constant interaction with people in pursuit of bringing the Gospel to bear on their lives.

LAY COMMITMENT AND OWNERSHIP: Excellence in ministry is not a one-person show. Even with vigorous and dynamic pastoral leadership, long-term excellence in faithfully carrying out the mission of the Gospel occurs only where the laity are committed to the vision of what their congregation's ministry can be. In the excellent churches, the laity "own," take responsibility for and are trusted with carrying out the work of the people of God.

The Expressions of Excellence

QUALITY WORSHIP: Centering the community's life and source of strength in Word and Sacrament, worship becomes a driving desire to speak and do the Gospel in a way which clearly communicates to the hopes and fears of people today and nurtures the faith of the worshipping community.

QUALITY EDUCATION: It is aimed at seeing that members, especially adults(!), are biblically and theologically literate in order that they might know what it means to be Christians in today's world and witness effectively.

QUALITY CARE AND OUTREACH: This includes both the care of members in the congregation by the pastor and fellow members and the service and witness ministries of the congregation, both to its local community and, through the whole Body of Christ, the world.

Reading this, some might say there is nothing new under the sun. Obviously, others have said this before. For example, a study of the 100 congregations in the Lutheran church in America which increased in worship attendance by 30 percent or more revealed many of these same qualities at work in effective ministry.[6] To some degree all of the above are present in every congregation—some poorly so, in other churches in a mediocre or even fairly good way. In dynamic, lively congregations, however, the above are done excellently. Both pastors and laypeople have a clear sense of their mission as a church which is biblically and confessionally grounded.

The key words in the above are excellence and quality. Borrowing the words of the Trinity, Camp Hill, Pennsylvania's, mission statement, strong pastors and congregations are committed to ". . .seeking excellence in all our ministries." They seek to be faithful to God's call by seeking excellence in all they do.

Before describing the above in more detail I must issue a disclaimer. Nowhere in this book will you find a clear-cut, fool-proof, so-many-step formula for church growth. Despite all the junk churches receive in the mail or which sits on Christian bookstore shelves claiming to be the magic solution for whatever ails your church, I must assert that *there is no magic. There are no special formulas, programs, gimmicks, or techniques for getting your church to grow.* Perhaps there is for creating some slick, glitzy, successful religious enterprise, but not for carrying out a faithful ministry of the Gospel—which is biblically and confessionally what the church is to be about. There is only the plain vanilla, down-to-earth, real person-to-person doing of the themes mentioned above. The key ingredient is not even the themes, but the commitment to do them well. "Excellence in ministry" is not competitive superiority over other congregations, but a consistent dedication to what faithfulness demands in doing the ministry of the Gospel. What happens in parishes which excel in ministry is that they do the very simple, common tasks of ministry uncommonly well. In some cases, numerical growth results—which should not surprise us. But, in the end, that is not the main thing. As Rev. David Gleason wrote to me upon entering the ministry, all that matters and all that God asks of us is that we be faithful. To seek to be faithful is to seek excellence in ministry.

CHAPTER II

The Foundations of Excellence: Mission

One of the great fad-words in the church in recent years has been "mission." It gets used all the time, often to cover a multitude of causes (sins?). Pastors preach about having a "sense of mission." Congregations prepare "mission statements" to describe their ministry. It has become a common catch-word for fund-raising appeals: In the 1970s the Lutheran Church in America had "Strength For Mission Appeal"; now we have "One in Mission." Just because we use the term, however, does not imply that we agree universally on its meaning. Confusion abounds at all levels of the church. Pastor Neal Boese of the Michigan Synod (LCA) recalls asking the question, "What is the mission of the church?" at one of his Evangelism Institutes and getting back at least a dozen different opinions on the subject. Asking the same question of seminary faculty, he got a similar response.

If confusion and jingoism mark the church's general understanding of mission, it certainly did not in the congregations of this study. These churches conveyed a clear notion of who they were and what God wanted them to do, and they did it. This, in the simplest terms, is what mission is all about. It is what one writer has called "identity in action":

> Mission in this biblical sense is ... 'identity in action.' The accent does not lie upon programs and strategies, quotas and statistics, but rather on a vital, functioning identity. There are no bifurcations in the biblical understanding, no tension between witness and service, and no grappling with definitions; the problem is one of uncomplicated perception of identity.[1]

These churches excelled in ministry because they knew their mission and did it. Their sense of mission as "identity in action" was evident in the way they described themselves, and there was nothing fancy or elaborate or theologically sophisticated in the way they went about it. Some had developed well-thought-out written mission statements; yet even these always revolved around basic themes which were common to the other excellent churches. In fact, the great strength of all these churches' sense of mission was a focus on the basics of worship, education, and outreach. "All ministry is really very basic," commented Pastor Scott Ickert of Leesburg, Virginia. Indeed it is, as these churches described it: to be a worshipping community centered in Word and Sacrament, to live for the purpose of bringing the Gospel to the unchurched, to evidence God's love by caring service to the needs of others. The congregations varied only in their concrete expression of these basics in their particular situations.

Accompanying this sense of mission were strong values which permeated congregational life and guided the way they lived out their mission. In many cases these became the reason for their reputation—their "long suit" in the community, as Pastor Richard Dowhower described it. For example: "Everyone in D.C. knows what Luther Place is," remarked Pastor John Steinbruck, "We are the church that opens its doors for the homeless."

Again, there was nothing fancy or frilly about the values these pastors and laity talked about, just basic stuff:

"We concentrate on the fundamentals. . . ." said Pastor Lehman of Trinity Lutheran, Lancaster, "basic pastoral work, preaching with substance and content, meaningful worship, content-oriented education, evangelism, and social ministry outreach."

"Our first order of business was to be a community of prayer," said Rev. David Hunsberger of his ministry at St. John's Church in Fairfield, Pennsylvania.

Basic biblical hospitality characterizes Luther Place in Washington, D.C.

Music in worship, education and pastoral care described Trinity Lutheran Church, Camp Hill, Pennsylvania.

Other responses were similar: "Being Lutheran, we don't apologize for our roots," said Peter Rudowski of Cincinnati. Respondents consistently described these roots as a focus on grace ("our Johnny one-note," said one pastor) and the unity of Word and Sacrament ministry. "Did you have any special program that you used to get Emmanuel Church to grow?" I asked Rev. John Cochran of his 12-year ministry there. "Only one," he said. "Sunday Mass. Always, always: Word and Sacrament." In fact, peculiarly absent in interviews with these churches was the description of mission as implementing a strategy for growth, a collection of programs, or achieving statistical goals. Instead, time and again, there was expressed a desire to do the tasks of ministry well. "We seek excellence in all our ministries," read the conclusion of Trinity, Camp Hill's mission statement. In truth, it describes the commitment which is at work in any lively ministry.

Going into this study I expected to find a great emphasis placed on how the congregation was structured internally. This, surprisingly, turned out not to be the case. Organizational structure varied tremendously from congregation to congregation. Some churches, especially the larger ones, had highly developed structures with detailed manuals of committee guidelines which were used to educate and assist committees in doing their work. Others, even in above-average size congregations, resorted to ad-hoc task forces to do the work of the congregation instead of constantly trying to maintain a committee system: "What needs doing gets done," said Rev. John Freed of Holy Spirit Lutheran Church in West Bloomfield, Michigan. "We just get a group of people to do it. We emphasize the job over the structure." Still others, especially in rural situations, found the traditional committee system unnecessary to getting things done. Said Pastor Hunsberger, "I found we didn't need a Social Ministry committee in our small town; a communication network already existed which kept tabs on people who needed help and generated responses of its own. All I had to do was watch out for people who might be slipping through the cracks." Pastor Myron Herzberg in Remsen, Iowa, observed: "When I came here, I noticed that the church did not have a highly-developed committee structure, but I decided not to institute one until I understood why this was so. After understanding why, I also knew that I didn't need to institute one."

So, organizational structures varied from church to church. "Structure follows strategy," one pastor observed. It develops as a means of doing the tasks of ministry in a given setting. To be sure, in almost all responses there was an emphasis on good planning and implementation, but the structures used to carry out the plans and programs varied from tight- to loose-knit. Two factors tended to influence what structure churches adopted. First, organizational structure was a function of size. "The big church simply is different," said Pastor Richard Dowhower. A whole different set of dynamics is at work. The larger the congregation, the greater the need for a strong organization to do the many things that need to get done. The large church needs to find a way to provide the small group face-to-face contact and relationship development among members—something that may occur naturally in small churches where everyone knows one another.

The other factor that influenced structure is location. My own observation from serving congregations in suburban and rural settings is that the need to maintain small group life is less critical in a rural church. Such small groups tend to exist in the local community because people commonly see each other in non-church settings during the week. In suburban congregations, however, members often have no contact during the week. Thus, the organizational life—committees, groups, etc.—of these churches provides a setting for the personal contact that occurs naturally between members in rural locations (and, in truth, in the street neighborhoods of the inner city) through local community events, in restaurants, stores, banks, barber shops, and other places of business. In general, the larger and more suburban a congregation is, the greater the need for organizational structures to provide the setting for relationships to develop. In a sense, the organizational life of a large congregation enables it to be a collection of small churches, providing and nurturing the values of strong personal relationships, intimacy, and member cohesion which is the great strength of smaller, rural parishes.

Yet, regardless of the variety in organizational structure, what was present in all of these churches was a strong emphasis and understanding of mission, fueled by a set of values which encapsulated the congregation's understanding of its mission and provided the motivating power for doing the tasks of ministry.

So, what is holding churches back today? A regular question in the interview process was, "What are the negative forces and factors working against congregations achieving excellence in ministry?" The common response? Surprisingly, only a few mentioned the cultural forces today pitted against the church's work. Not often did people talk about values of society being against those of Christianity. Indeed, just the opposite was the case. Observed Pastor Cochran, "I find people surprisingly open to the Gospel. . . . They almost dare you to talk about it." Most saw the problem as spiritual, not material or cultural. "Ill-defined sense of mission" typified their response. "A church must have a vision of itself as the called-out *(ecclesia)* people of God, rooted in Word and Sacrament, and be clear as to what it is to be about," commented Pastor Mark Radecke of Christ Lutheran Church, Roanoke. "If it doesn't, all it becomes is a social agency or religious Elk's club."

A clear understanding of mission—knowing who you are and what God is calling you to do—is the first and clearly indispensable foundation of a church, indeed, *the* church. By nature it is grounded in and informed by the church's biblical and confessional tradition. It isn't something which has to be developed *ex nihilo* or *de novo*. It isn't "found" through some committee process. "We don't debate the Great Commission (Matt. 28:19-20)," remarked Rev. David Gleason. "We simply do it." Again, it gets back to the congregation having a clear identity and purpose (knowing who you are and what you are to be about): "The problem with too many churches today," added Pastor Dick Bieber of Messiah Lutheran Church, Detroit, "is that they are not focused on the person of Jesus. They're too distracted into becoming 'agencies' with 'clients' or withdrawn into clubs for nice people."

Just what can a renewed, focused mission do for the life of a congregation? Time and again I listened to stories of pastors who came to dismal, dying situations and, by simply devoting themselves to doing Word and Sacrament ministry, saw great turn-arounds in their parishes. Pastor Richard Neuhaus came to St. John's the Evangelist Church, Brooklyn, in 1961, against the wishes of ecclesiastical officials who wanted to close it down. Seventeen years later he left it a church of 900 communicant members. The secret? A commitment to the basic work of the church, worship, with, he added, "a lot of sheer, unvarnished enthusiasm for what we were about there." Pastor Dee Littleton came to St. Paul's Lutheran Church, Lansdowne, Pennsylvania, after it had suffered through several disastrous or short-term pastorates. Attendance was in the low fifties and people viewed her pastorate as a "make-it or break-it" time for the church. Four years later attendance has doubled due to, she said, moving from a survival outlook to a mission focus. In a similar vein Larry Smoose of God's Love Lutheran Church, Newtown, Pennsylvania, described how his congregation moved from a small church with a low self-image to the fastest-growing church in their area by focusing on what God calls the church to be—with goals to implement what their mission calls them to do. Certainly one of the great success stories when discussing the importance of mission for the church—and a story which has become the model for similar ventures in inner-city ministry in other areas—is the story of Center City Lutheran Parish of Philadelphia (CCLP). By the early sixties the once-prosperous immigrant Lutheran churches of Philadelphia were retreating on all fronts as their constituents moved to the suburbs and neighborhoods changed. In the decades after 1930, nineteen congregations were disbanded; another five (including one which merged with a congregation in Clifton Heights, Pennsylvania, in 1959 that I served from 1978-1985) joined the others. A sense of despair and imminent death pervaded the pastors and members of the inner city churches. By the early 1960's most church officials predicted many of the churches would close within ten years.

Then in 1964 Center City Lutheran Parish, a coalition ministry among these churches, was founded to foster the renewal of Lutheran congregations in inner city Philadelphia. Its first director was Pastor Robert Neumeyer. His program for redeveloping the congregations was very simple and basic. "First," he said, "We are not closing any more churches in Philadelphia"—and he got the financial backing to prevent it. Second, congregations would minister to their neighborhoods instead of chasing yesterday's members all over the suburbs. To this end pastors, too, would be required to live in their church's neighborhood. No longer would they have the luxury of commuting in from the "outer space" of the suburbs. Word and Sacrament would be the focus of the life of each parish. Pastors' meetings were held each week to foster collegiality, instead of competition, and the sharing of mutual joys and sorrows. A variety of programs and services to pastors, congregations and neighborhoods were developed to assist them in strengthening their common and individual ministries.

Within two years Neumeyer had replaced 95 percent of the pastors in the churches of CCLP. Since 1964 no church in CCLP has closed; the two that did not join the coalition in 1964, however, did. Under Neumeyer's leadership, until his death in 1978, and that of his successor, Pastor John Cochran, the decline in the churches bottomed out in the early 1970s. Since then, the overall pattern—with a year now and then of losses—has been one of growth. In looking back on twenty-plus years of CCLP, Pastor Cochran remarked on one of the basic things they discovered, or better, reaffirmed, in doing mission. His statement reflects what Pastor Neuhaus said about evangelism occurring through the church when the church is the church and about mission as "identity in action":

> One was the realization that we are most effective in ministry when we are most true to our churchly identity, when we place the living presence of Jesus in Word and Sacrament at the center of every day, every week, every activity, every work of mercy, every advocacy.[2]

All this talk about the importance of a sense of mission really should not be too surprising. Christianity has been from the start a mission-oriented religion, by our Lord's command (Matthew 28:18-20). Emil Brunner earlier in this century expressed it in his well-known saying, "The church exists by mission, just as fire exists by burning."[3] A focus on mission, then, is the heart and soul of a church's life. Without it a congregation dies, just as Jesus has indicated in Mark 8:34-35: ". . . If anyone would come after me, he must deny himself and take up his cross and follow me. For whoever wants to save his life will lose it, but whoever loses his life for me and for the gospel will save it."

The opposite to this clear sense of mission, or rather its perversion, is mission defined as institutional survival. Once such an outlook sets into a parish, it is difficult to eradicate. When the "bottom line" becomes numerical growth it poisons the atmosphere of a congregation, infecting the people with a self-centered outlook on new members, on spending, on how changes are received. This squelches creativity. My first diagnosis of this congregational illness came in early 1979 in my first church. Preparing a sermon on Isaiah 42:1-7, the Old Testament reading for the Baptism of Jesus, I became aware of the contrast between God's calling his people to service, even in adverse circumstances, and the kinds of comments I'd been hearing in my first year at that parish. In one way or another, the comments all had a common theme: "What do we have to do to 'make it'?" The people were not asking service or mission questions, but survival questions.

Other pastors described the same phenomenon to me. Rev. John Steinbruck remarked that when he first came to Luther Place Church in 1970, parishioners were worrying about how the church would survive in its hostile neighborhood. "We struggled over the issue and our unique calling in that place," he said, "like Jacob wrestling at the river Jabbok with the Lord. Then, one night, it knocked on our door in the form of one of the street people seeking shelter from the cold. The answer, simply, was to let them in. So began our renewal in mission, and we've never worried about survival since. In fact, that of which we were most suspicious and afraid—the surrounding neighborhood—became God's gift to us to revitalize our life."

Said Pastor Greg Pile of New Centerville, Pennsylvania, on this same topic, "A significant negative factor in any church is a survival mentality. It may work for the short term, but not in the long run. The congregation has to root itself in God's call, not in what is best for them in a narrow, institutionally self-serving sense."

Indeed, the two biggest survival worries of many pastors and their congregations—members and money (bodies and bucks)—simply was not an end these churches pursued. In fact, in quite a few it was not an issue at all. Doing the task of ministry well was the issue. And, lo and behold, the members and the money took care of themselves. The classic comment on this came from Pastor

John Siefken of Prince of Glory Lutheran Church in Madison
Heights, Michigan. When he became pastor in 1969, the church was
terribly divided, debt-ridden, and almost bankrupt. Recalled John,
"People would ask me, 'What are you going to do about that huge
$100,000 debt?' I told them that I wasn't going to do anything about
it. I wasn't even going to think about it, or I'd never get anything
done. Instead, we focused on good worship, good teaching, good
outreach, and hoped the debt would go away." They did, and it did.
My intern pastor in Cincinnati, Rev. Peter Rudowski, put it just as
unabashedly: "Congregations don't need to do fund-raising. Do the
ministry consistently well and the money will be there." People join
a church and support it financially not in order to see it survive, but
because they believe in its cause.

   The survival syndrome is not the only factor crippling congregations in their ministry today. There are those not-so-rare cases
where a church really does not want to grow, where it has become
so turned in on itself that by its actions, if not always by its words, it
says to people, "We don't want your kind here." It is an odd and
perverted sense of mission, but it happens. Rev. Rudowski of Good
Shepherd Church believes this problem occurs when a congregation focuses on its own internal needs, wants, and goals (the traditional theological term for this is sin) and closes itself to the
changes occuring in its local environment and its needs for ministry
(see further comments below).

   The most blatant examples of this, of course, are in parishes
undergoing racial and ethnic change in their communities. My first
congregation, St. Marks-Temple of Clifton Heights, Pennsylvania,
came into being through a 1959 merger. One branch of the merger
was a white-flight congregation from West Philadelphia. It was not
hard to see why they could not make it in their former neighborhood. In the early 1950s the church Council simply voted that no
blacks could become members of their church. Other churches use
more ingenious methods. The now-defunct St. Marcus congregation
kept undesirables out by keeping its front sign in German—ten
years after they had gone to English-language services. In his response to my questionnaire, Pastor Steve Rode of Christ Lutheran,
San Antonio, identified a key negative force working against a
church achieving excellence in ministry as ". . . a lack of vision in
identifying the needs of its community." The examples above provide a sad confirmation of his observation.

   More frequently, however, the way a congregation turns inward
is less blatant. It occurs in a very subtle, disguised way. Few
churches, if any, consciously and intentionally set out to lose their
sense of mission or turn it inward upon themselves in self-serving

ways. Pastor Peter Rudowski pointed out how the tendency to turn inward and become self-focused often occurs in the way a parish does its planning. He explained that even though the planning process may be undertaken with a desire to improve the congregation's exercise of its ministry, questions asked often determine the focus and real concerns of the parish, whether it will be inward or outward in its vision of ministry. A common tendency in recent years in many congregations has been to use an "MBO" ("Management-By-Objectives") approach. The congregation begins by asking the question, "What do we want to accomplish in the next year (or any other time period)?" The congregation's future is extrapolated on the basis of its present condition and the interests of the members. Such a focus is self-centered. It does not ask questions about what is going on in the parish's environment, how that environment is changing, the implications of those changes for its ministry, and how, in light of what God calls the church to be, the parish can best minister to its environment. Focusing on the environment in which the church finds itself, on the other hand, sets before the parish the future God prepares for his people and begins to allow them to struggle with how that calling in Christ will take shape.

The importance of a church's mission to the environment in which it dwells is nowhere better expressed than in Jeremiah's word to God's people during their exile in Babylon: "Thus says the Lord of hosts, the God of Israel . . . seek the welfare of the city where I have sent you into exile, and pray to the Lord on its behalf, for in its welfare you will find your welfare" (Jer. 29.7). Having such a sense of mission makes all the difference in whether a church reaches out and lives or turns in upon itself and dies. Two congregations in North Philadelphia reveal the difference between these two stances. I call their stories "A Tale of Two Churches." At St. Simeon's Lutheran Church, despite the change of their neighborhood from German to black, Hispanic and Asian peoples, the parish has not retreated into itself. Instead, under the pastorates of first Rev. Edward Miller and now Rev. Tim Ohlmann, the church has vigorously sought to minister to the people of its neighborhood. Today all four racial/ethnic groups are found in its membership, and the services are done in English, Spanish, and the Laotian Hmong language. That is the good news story. The bad news story is of another Lutheran church just two blocks away. Though it had far greater financial resources than St. Simeon's, the congregation was hamstrung when it came to considering how it might reach out to its neighborhood. Barricading itself behind its doors, the congregation eventually dwindled to a handful of members all related to one another, utterly closed off to anyone not related to them. A few years ago it closed its doors for good. The final testimony to its utter lack of mission focus and calling to be stewards of the Gospel was a proposal put forward by some of the members to divide the financial resources of the church among themselves! The building, ironically, was sold to an Hispanic Seventh-Day Adventist congregation. The people from the neighborhood got in after all.

In describing his ministry in Brooklyn in particular and the church's ministry in general, Richard Neuhaus wrote:

> The purpose of the church is to sight, signal, support, and celebrate the coming of the Kingdom. Having sighted that coming in Christ, the church is to signal it in word and life. As a sacrament, (a "visible Word of God," to use Augustine's definition—ed.), the church symbolizes the future of the whole of humankind.[4]

This sense of mission is what breaks or makes a congregation. Rooted in our biblical and confessional tradition and clearly articulated through a value-system which permeates every level of the congregation, the missionary drive of the Gospel energizes people, regardless of their location, to do the tasks of ministry. Such congregations know who they are and what God wants them to do. They do it well. That is the difference.

CHAPTER III

The Foundations of Excellence: Pastoral Leadership

"The greatest variable in a congregation is the pastor. A congregation is basically stuck with its location and its members, and from one pastor to the next these change little or only gradually. Yet, over the course of several pastors one person's ministry will stand out, while the rest will be so-so at best. The ministry of a good pastor can, despite poor location and passive members, make a church come alive during the years he or she is there."

Rev. Peter Rudowski of Cincinnati, Ohio, tacked this comment on to the end of his questionnaire response. It points clearly to the critical necessity of pastoral leadership in achieving excellence in the parish. "The truth is," wrote Rev. Richard Neuhaus in *Freedom For Ministry*, "that there is scarcely a local church that has a sense of lively celebration and mission that does not also have strong pastoral leadership. Strong pastors do not always have lively churches, but lively churches, almost without exception, have strong pastors."[1] This is not to minimize the importance of committed lay leadership in a church, which will be treated in the next chapter. This section, however, will focus on the unique place pastoral leadership has in a congregation, how it is exercised, and critical issues facing ordained ministers today in fulfilling this leadership role.

What is pastoral leadership? I asked everyone I interviewed this question: "How does a pastor exercise leadership in the congregation?" As I listened to the answers, consistently they fell into the four "strategies of leadership" described by Warren Bennis and Bert Nanus in their book, *Leaders: The Strategies For Taking Charge*. Briefly, these are:

1. The capturing of the attention of members of the organization through the creation of a *vision* of what their organization is called to be and can do.

2. *Communicating* the vision clearly so that it becomes more than just the personal belief of the leader, but a shared vision of the future among all members at every level in the organization.

3. Developing *trust* between followers and leaders by engaging in predictable, reliable, accountable actions. Referred to as "positioning" by Bennis and Nanus, this means knowing and exhibiting a clear sense of who you are and what you are about which builds an identity in the organization and its environment which people know and can depend on over time.

4. Raising the level of self-esteem in the organization as a whole and individuals in particular through *positive self-regard:* capitalizing on one's strengths, nurturing skills, focusing on succeeding.[2]

These "strategies" of taking charge are, according to Bennis and Nanus, the key factors in successful leadership and the pivotal force behind successful organizations. They create a vision for the organization and mobilize its resources and people to strive for the realization of their hoped-for future.[3] All four of these strategies were found in the comments the pastors and laity made about the work of the pastor in attaining excellence in parish ministry.

Vision was the word used with almost boring repetition by clergy and laity alike in describing the leadership role of the pastor. Rather than describe what they said, I'll let them speak for themselves:

"A pastor provides a vision of a Christ-centered community," wrote back a layperson from St. John's Lutheran Church, Des Moines, Iowa.

"A key problem many pastors have in their parishes today is their inability to articulate a vision and purpose to their people about the church," said Pastor Bob Holley of Charlottesville, Virginia.

Pastor Greg Pile of New Centerville Parish, Pennsylvania, added: "Problems arise when a pastor only says what the people want to hear, instead of challenging people to a broader vision of ministry."

I asked Carol Jarvis of God's Love Church in Newtown, Pennsylvania, why she thought her pastor, Rev. Larry Smoose, was so effective. Her reply: "He is a leader with authority and a sense of mission."

In looking back on his ministry at St. John's Church in Brooklyn, Pastor Richard Neuhaus remarked, "We simply had raw, unvarnished excitement about the ministry and what that congregation could do. . . . I regarded it then and now as the most important work in the world."

From Roanoke, Virginia, Pastor Mark Radecke observed: "The pastor as leader sets the vision for the church . . . without a vision, the people perish" (cf. Proverbs 29:18).

Rev. Neal Boese said: "The pastor's job follows the mission of the church. He or she is called to mobilize, to energize and to unleash the congregation to reach out to the unchurched."

Pastor Jon Holmer, Hope Lutheran Church, Midland, Texas said: "The pastor must be able to give a sense of vision and guidance to the people, and instill hope and enthusiasm for the ministry."

In the previous chapter it was noted how a renewed sense of mission can turn a moribund congregation into a place where a lively, dynamic ministry of the Gospel is carried out. From the comments of the people above—which are just a sample of the responses I received—it is clear that pastoral leadership is a key factor in creating a lively sense of mission. Rarely does a church grow in its ministry without it, just as sheep without a shepherd (Latin: *pastor*) are lost.

"A pastor provides the vision of a Christ-centered community," wrote the layperson from Des Moines mentioned above. To which his pastor, Rev. Jerry Schmalenberger, added: "He or she must communicate that vision constantly in preaching, in face-to-face conversation and by intense commitment and personal example." Communicating the vision of what a church can be goes hand-in-hand with having one. It is a constant endeavor. "I use every opportunity to teach the faith—not just in class or services, but in meetings and informal settings as well," noted Pastor Pile. "The squeaky wheel gets the grease," wrote Pastor William Derrick from his parish in Brenham, Texas, "so I communicate my concerns to the people as often as I can." When I asked Pastor David Deal of Trinity Church in Yeadon, Pennsylvania, how his church was not only surviving, but growing, through a racial transition in the neighborhood, David said, "I have just constantly made it clear to the congregation that we are an inclusive church that ministers to the people in this community."[4]

I would hasten to add at this point that the vision one communicates to one's parish goes beyond its geographical boundaries. It must embrace the one, holy, catholic and apostolic church. The pastors I talked to were anything but the "Lone Ranger" types who, in typical Protestant fashion, viewed their churches as their own synods with themselves as bishops. They all revealed in their words and deeds a concern for the wider ministry of the church. Pastor Bob Holley of Epiphany Lutheran in Dale City, Virginia, reported how many people in his congregation were shocked when he suggested that the congregation provide assistance to a new Lutheran mission congregation in town. His attitude was not to hold that church at arm's length, but to embrace it. In Des Moines, Iowa, Rev. Jerry Schmalenberger's church went even further. His church raised funds to help a new Pentecostal rescue mission for the homeless get off the ground. Such actions remind congregations that the Body of Christ extends beyond their four walls. It builds a vision of being part of a universal community of faith transcending human distinctions and divisions (Gal. 3:26-29).

It is important to remember, too, that communicating the vision to the parish is not just a matter of talking a lot about it. Most effective communication is *non-verbal*. It comes from what we see, not from what we hear. Pastors ought to be mindful of this. A pastor demonstrates her priorities in ministry and vision for her parish not just by what she says, but by what she does. The office of ministry is a public office in which visible, symbolic actions demonstrate to people what the pastor believes in. "I don't buy into this notion of the minister as an 'enabler' of people," said Rev. David Hunsberger. "It's become a cop-out for waiting for the laity to do things, for sitting in the office and waiting for them to come to you to be helped. My Marine Corps background won't let me do that. Leadership has to be by example, with the pastor out front. The office of ministry is a teaching office; a 'show and tell,' or better yet, 'tell and show' job." Through public actions the pastor communicates the values of the faith. This is especially so in the first months after a pastor begins work in a parish, when people are watching every move she makes to discern patterns which reveal her commitments and priorities in ministry.[5]

It has become commonplace in recent years to hear pastors bemoan the powerless position they have been placed in society today due to the growth of radio and TV media. Not a few wonder if they are effective at all. I would suggest, however, that most pastors simply do not realize that every day they are given innumerable opportunities to demonstrate their corcerns about the faith and to communicate their vision of the church to members and non-members alike. Every conversation, every action is watched by people for a clue to what the pastor regards as important in ministry.

Therefore, it is critically necessary for the pastor to become, as Dr. Robert Benne, Professor of Religion at Roanoke College, wrote, ". . . *very* intentional about what he or she does in the ministry." One can be sure that the message will not be lost on the people. Demonstrate a commitment to excellence in preaching, worship, teaching, outreach and pastoral care, and people will take notice. They also will take just as much notice of the opposite, as a layperson observed: "I am not sure if our new pastor knows what he is doing or wants to do here. The one thing he does seem to be clear about is getting in his two off days a week."

A bit of my own history at my current parish provides a case in point. I live in a one-intersection town in the heart of Pennsylvania apple country. My home sits atop a hill overlooking the intersection. On one corner sits a small restaurant. The first thing I did on my first day of work in the new parish was eat breakfast in that restaurant, introducing myself to the workers and patrons there. Several times each week I stop there for morning coffee or a meal and to talk with the people, most of whom are growers. The net effect of all this has been that people know I am available and interested in them and that my ministry in this area will be one of outreach to people. Hanging out at that restaurant also presented me numerous opportunities to witness to the Christian faith and to talk with people about issues from a Christian perspective— opportunities I would not have had if I were content to limit myself only to the educational offerings of our parish program.

It is often said that pastors live in goldfish bowls. Most resent it. The smart ones embrace it. They know that every moment of every day is an opportunity to show people what they are really concerned about.

Vision and its communication through word and deed are what pastoral leadership is about. Such leadership, as Nanus and Bennis point out, is different from *managing,* which has been the focus of most books on the practice of ministry in recent years. Their comments are worth noting here:

> By focusing attention on a vision, the leader operates on the *emotional* and *spiritual* resources of the organization, on its values, commitment, and aspirations. The manager, by contrast, operates on the *physical* resources of the organization, on its capital, human skills, raw materials, and technology.[6]

Go back to the comment Pastor Neal Boese made about the work of the pastor: ". . . to mobilize, energize, and unleash the congregation. . . ." That is the creation and communication of a vision

for the local parish. It implies that the pastor has to know clearly
what she is called to do in a congregation and is able to get that
message across to the people in visible, understandable ways. It is
the exact opposite of the management mentality, which has afflicted
both business corporations and churches in the last generation,
which is more concerned with the production of programs (which
are often addressed to needs that really aren't there, said one layperson), maintaining an organizational structure, gathering and as-
sessing reports and evaluations, reducing conflict, and institutional
efficiency. Our predilection for the latter has resulted in a situation
lamented by Pastor Cochran: "We've become a generation of tinker-
ers. We want to tinker with the liturgy, we want to tinker with the
mimeograph, we want to tinker with the committee structure, we
want to tinker . . . but we don't want to get out there and talk to
unbelievers about the Gospel"—which is what Jesus told his followers to do. And they did.

To be clear, however, these same pastors and laity cited the
need for ministers to be good administrators and executors of plans
as a key ingredient in ministry. They frequently cited poor administration as a major failing of pastors today:

> "Our pastor just does not know how to run an office, and as a
> result things are not getting done that have to be done," one
> layperson said.

> "Some pastors are simply inept when it comes to organization,
> administration, finance, and management," said Pastor Schmalen-
> berger, Des Moines, Iowa.

> Pat Smith of God's Love, Newtown, Pennsylvania, said: "Though
> most clergy work hard, some have not learned how to be ad-
> ministrators or how to use their time to the best advantage. . . .
> Some clergy do not plan ahead or see far enough 'down the
> road' to help their congregation to do so."

In my preparation for ministry, I was fortunate enough to have
an intern pastor who stressed the importance of administration as a
key factor in effective ministry. (These skills were certainly not
taught in the seminary curricula.) His lament was that too many pastors don't want to take the time and effort to do it. Yet, he stressed,
it is the means through which the pastor translates the concerns expressed in preaching and teaching into action in the parish, where
the vision gets implemented into concrete expression. Or, as Dave
Houck, a layperson, said about developing excellence in ministry,

"Telling it won't produce it." Action—envisioned, planned, and executed—will.

There are those, of course, who chide pastors for being concerned about administration because it is of lesser importance than preaching, teaching and administering sacraments. There are those purists who have a "minimalist" view of ministry as *only* preaching, teaching and leading worship, and that if one simply does these things, automatically *(ex opere operato!)* people will flock to church and all will be well in the congregation. Pastoral leadership is not a matter of doing the "minimum requirements" and expecting the rest to happen by magic. It rests on the total activities of the pastor in preaching and teaching the Gospel's promises. Administration is one area, and a very important one at that, in which this happens. Rather than being antithetical, these pastoral activities are complementary. Their linkage was best described in the comments of Pastor Smoose:

> Every pastor and congregation does planning and goal-setting in one way or another. The key difference is whether the goals are 'fuzzy' and hidden from the membership as a whole, or clearly set forth, visibly defined, known and implemented.

Administration is part of, not apart from or against, the pastor's work of ". . . holding up a vision, and calling forth and inspiring people to accomplish the vision," said Pastor Smoose.

Several other important qualities and attributes contribute to lively pastoral leadership. Characteristic of these pastors was a focus on the basics of ministry. These pastors were action-oriented and value-driven, focusing on the essential work of ministry and getting it done. Wrote Tom Peters, "Attention is all there is. . . . It's how you use your calendar to pay attention to what is important."[7] In the same vein Ed Saling, Director of Southeast Delaware District Lutheran Parish (another coalition ministry modeled on the Center City Lutheran Parish) observed, "The thing I note about good pastors is that they have a no-frills approach to ministry. They just do the basics well." In the first place, they were parish-centered. They agreed with Rev. Neuhaus' assessment of the parish ministry of Word and Sacrament ". . . as the most important work in the world." "What would you say to a pastor to help him develop his ministry in his situation?" I asked Pastor John Steinbruck of Washington, D.C. His concise reply was very simple, yet demanding in practice: "Get biblically oriented and community focused, and have the guts to work towards a faithful ministry." For Pastor Tim Ohlmann of Philadelphia, a sign posted on his desk reminds him everyday of the essential work he is to be about. It lists these as his job priorities:

PREACH

TEACH

VISIT

These pastors reflected their priorities in ministry by the way they used their time. Preaching, leading worship, teaching and visiting easily occupied two-thirds of their time. They regularly reported spending upwards of ten or more hours a week in teaching activities (including preparation) and twelve to eighteen in worship and preaching activity. Ninety-plus percent of their time was spent on activities in their parish. They resisted the temptation to "go off" to do ministry elsewhere, a temptation prevalent in the ministry and easy to fall into because of the appearance of "busyness" that it projects. I was warned of this by John Cochran before I began work in my first church. His words are still clear as a bell to me, "You will have to resist the tendency—and it will come from both your members and the church at large—to think that the real ministry is going on outside your parish area. Members will want you to go visit someone who lives miles outside the area your parish serves, and the national church will always be begging to have you serve on this committee or that task force. You've got to stay where you are and focus on ministry in your parish area."

Coupled with attention to the basics is the attribute of theological competence, mentioned by numerous pastors and laity as a key factor in effective ministry. Years ago, when I entered seminary, a professor said to the incoming class, "When you get in the parish, above all else people will expect you to know the Bible." The pastors of this study had a commitment to knowing the tradition of the faith. Their commitment was evidenced in the time they gave to continuing education; most gave at least three or more hours a week to it. They were lifelong learners, and sought ways to improve themselves: "I continually ask for and get evaluations of my ministry from my people," remarked Pastor Schmalenberger. By contrast, "fuzzy theology" and "poorly defined understanding of ministry" were often cited as negative factors working against effective ministry.

Competence, seriousness and intentionality" were Robert Benne's observations about what makes for lively pastoral ministry. In short, good pastors, like good churches, know who they are, what God expects them to do, and make the best use of their time in getting it done.

Technical expertise, however, is not the only ingredient in the making of effective pastoral leadership. There are certain personal qualities which figure in as well. Two major factors are enthusiasm and energy. It is safe to say that these pastors enjoyed their work and this joy was picked up by the members and translated into enthusiasm in their commitment to the mission of the church. "I like to have fun at what I do," Pastor Greg Wenhold of Good Shepherd Church, King of Prussia, Pennsylvania, unabashedly said. His enjoyment of the work of being a pastor has undoubtedly been a key to reversing a downward slide in that church a few years ago. "I would look for a person who enjoys being with people, who likes to 'mix it up' as a quality in selecting a pastor," mentioned another minister. A lay person, who during many years of service in the several churches has observed many pastors, said the good ones hold up church work not as a dull labor to be done out of obligation or necessity, but as fun. He told this story:

> I remember Pastor Ed Horn from when we belonged to Trinity Lutheran Church in Philadelphia. It was the time of year for the annual Every Member Visitation stewardship drive. Getting people for it is usually as easy as pulling teeth. I was asked for the first time to serve. But, when he talked to us in the training session, Pastor Horn did not talk about the need to raise money or even how much was needed. He talked about how much fun it was to meet people, to share the faith with them and get to know them. He presented the church as a believable cause, and said that we would have fun doing the church work we were being asked to do.

Yet, I must hasten to add that as much as enthusiasm and excitement for the work of ministry were mentioned by those in this study, no one said that having a certain type of personality was a prerequisite for the office of ministry. Only once did a respondent mention the need for the pastor to have "charisma." Indeed, the pastors with whom I talked were as diverse a group of people as anyone could find, from very outgoing to very laid-back types, from those who were very caustic and biting in their assessment of things to those who were consummate diplomats. Despite differences in personality, all had enthusiasm for the ministry and chided their fellow clergy for their negativism ("They bitch too much," said one) and pessimism ("That only repels people," commented another). Others simply said that some clergy are just too lazy: "I know a pastor who thinks he's put in a full day's work if he has run off the bulletin for the Sunday service," was one response. My response to that is to ask why a pastor would be running off a bulletin in the first place. A good pastor ought to know and distinguish in practice where the pastor's work ends and the secretary's begins. (Pastor Rudowski used to say, "Well, I'll do that work if they want me to, but I would also call to my church's attention that I am awfully expensive secretarial help, and wouldn't they like to consider a less-expensive alternative?")

It should be noted that zest, enthusiasm, and energy for ministry does not mean that these pastors lacked seriousness in their approach or had a glib, "Smile, Jesus loves you" response to the suffering they encountered. Enthusiasm and commitment were seen as complementary, not antagonistic: "This does not mean being a rah-rah person," said Pastor Mark Radecke, "but the pastor must convince the people that he believes all this stuff about the Gospel, and is excited about it."

In 1975 I was part of a group from my seminary that spent a month in East and West Germany studying the life of the church in those two countries. Coming from their background of a "Volkskirche" (state church) style of ecclesiastical organization in which clergy were paid by the "church tax" system (2 percent of one's income was collected by the state along with income taxes and distributed to the church), our West German hosts were curious about the American voluntary system in which clerical compensation is a direct result of free-will member offerings. Their comment was, "Since the local congregation pays your salary, you have to do and say as they command." In their minds this meant that clergy were forced to be subservient, unassertive and compliant in their exercise of the office of ministry. In truth, just the opposite is the case. Those interviewed in this study repeatedly stressed the need for the pastor to be assertive if he or she is to exercise effective leadership. As John Steinbruck indicated in his comment above, to be a pastor one has to have the *guts* to work toward a faithful ministry. It does not come easily, automatically, or to the pastor who sits back, waiting for others to take the lead. As John Cochran commented to me about trying to develop a new sense of ministry in a depressed parish, "Sometimes you just have to *will* it into existence, because sometimes people have to experience the positive effects of something before they will decide in favor of it."

I would hasten to add that assertiveness is not to be confused with an aggressive, domineering approach which steamrolls over people. Rather, it is the ability to be clear on what one is concerned about and willing to demonstrate those concerns to others verbally and in actions. It is what Bennis and Nanus call "picking an angle into the wind" and sticking to that angle with tireless persistence and dedication.[8]

Unfortunately, in conversations with pastors and laity a different attribute characterizes a good number of pastors today—that of passivity and lack of assertiveness. Some indicated to me that this begins in the approach one takes to seminary studies, whether there is a serious effort made to become a good student of the theological disciplines of the pastoral office, or whether one views seminary as simply a "trade school" to pick up a few skills to qualify for a job. During my final year in seminary a professor mentioned to me what he saw as the growing inclination to simply follow the agenda of the national church or the direction one saw other pastors and churches taking. Call it institutional buck-passing: One avoids taking a direct leadership position and instead becomes merely an information conduit for what everyone else says the church ought to be doing. That's hardly picking an angle into the wind and sticking with it, or having the guts to work towards a faithful ministry. Effective pastoral leadership requires a resistance to the "herd-instinct" and the willingness to see and pursue the unique way one is called to minister in a given setting. Said one pastor, "I will admit to being a bit of a maverick in the ministry. I don't buy into whatever is the current fad in the church or the latest 'big push' from headquarters, because inevitably that winds up being only part of the whole ministry the church is supposed to be doing." Or as John Steinbruck added to his comment above, "You gotta have *chuzpah,* and use your own creativity."

Inevitably, lack of assertiveness in the ministry relates to the way one approaches and responds to conflict in the parish. A frequently voiced comment about ineffective pastoral leadership was reluctance to take risks for fear of losses, resulting in a desire to simply maintain the status quo. "A pastor has to challenge people to seek excellence," wrote Pat Smith, "but some have a fear of trying to challenge people." Part of this, of course, is the natural human inclination to avoid conflict and maintain tranquility. But in its worst form the desire to avoid controversy and preserve harmony creates a sham peace which covers up the real issues facing a congregation. So, as an article in one religious periodical expressed it, we sweetly sing, "Blest Be the Tie That Binds, Our Hearts in Christian Love," yet in practice we carefully avoid anything that would test that tie, such as engaging in activities that reveal significant differences.[9] Pastors and laity in this study both saw the need for leaders in the church to have the courage to risk conflict in order to promote a vision of what their congregation could be. "I'll fight for, though not insist

on, what I believe in, and expect others to do the same," said one
pastor. "I believe pastors have to be willing to see conflict as an
opportunity to teach," said David Gleason. "Too often we don't take
advantage of these opportunities to teach, and if we go about it in a
manner that shows our care for the congregation, the people will
be responsive." Or, Dee Littleton's comment: "A pastor simply has
to be willing to face the issues, have the courage to confront people
when they engage in moaning and groaning, and focus their attention on the mission of the congregation." By and large, the issue is
not conflict itself, but the way one approaches it. Again, the courage
to be assertive about one's convictions is different from the aggressive drive to accomplish one's wishes at all costs. In most cases, if
issues are faced openly, out of visible care for the congregation, and
if people are listened to and their views respected, the congregation
will survive and grow even in conflict.

Having a vision, being able to communicate it, courage, enthusiasm, assertiveness, competence in theology and practice—all of
these are essential ingredients in the make-up of effective pastoral
leaders. Buttressing all of these, though, is a clear sense of one's
call to be a pastor in the place one is called to serve. This emphasis,
mentioned repeatedly in my contacts with pastors and laity, cannot
be understated. Again, the best way to describe this emphasis is
simply to let these pastors and laity speak for themselves:

"The greatest negative at work among clergy today is a lack of a
sense of a divine call to ministry," wrote back Rev. Jerry Schmalenberger. He described this divine call in a 1986 article in *The
Lutheran* as the ". . . go-power out of which Moses, Paul and
thousands of clergy have operated. . . . We have lost among Lutherans the strong sense of God's call to the ordained ministry."[10]

"The pastor is one who does not see his or her life apart from
the biblical story," said Rev. Mark Radecke.

"Are you willing to treat the ministry as a call from God, to lay
down your life for the people and community you serve?" asked
Rev. John Cochran.

"Our basic problems as pastors are spiritual," said Pastor Richard
Bieber. "They have to do with the questions 'Who am I?' and
'Why am I here?' They have to do with one's call to be a pastor."

I would hazard a conclusion at this point: It is only when one
sees oneself as under a bone-deep sense of a divine call to ministry

that one can have a vision of one's own ministry and communicate that to one's congregation. On this point, there must be a great coherence between our theological convictions and the practice of ministry. Classical Lutheranism, in the catholic tradition of the church, understood the pastoral office as one divinely instituted. That is, its legitimacy, validity and strength comes not as an invention of the church, but from God:

> To obtain such faith, God instituted the office of ministry; that is, provided the Gospel and the sacraments.[11]

It is God himself who instituted and, therefore, defines the office of ministry, not the church. This character of the pastoral office as divinely instituted works to provide the pastor with his or her source of confidence, freedom and guidance for ministry. Regardless of the pastor's personal reasons for wanting to be a minister, regardless of her feelings of adequacy for the job, his doubts about continuation in the ministry, or the worth of her efforts, the fact remains that at all times the pastor is called by God to exercise the office of ministry, and it is God, not the pastor or anyone else, who makes the final declaration of value about a pastor's efforts.[12]

A few years ago a very fine, now-retired pastor, William Elbert of Springfield, Pennsylvania, commented to a group of us recently-ordained ministers, "The worst thing I see happening in the ministry today is a lack of a sense of being called. Without the conviction of God's call to ministry, pastors tend to serve self rather than God. They are unwilling to live in the belief that God's grace is sufficient for those who would serve him." The pastors in this survey frequently chided the growth of careerism and professionalism among the ordained as factors working against excellence in ministry. It apparantly begins at the seminary level: "I was amazed," said Pastor Ohlmann, "at the way some of my classmates only talked of their call in terms of their package." He went on to lament the effects of careerism he has seen among the clergy: spending only two to three years at a call and lack of commitment to, and sometimes even disdain for, the people clergy serve. Myron Herzberg in Iowa echoed these comments: "I see pastors who are just too self-centered, who won't put themselves on the line, who do only what is rewarding to themselves and not to the community they are called to serve." Speaking out of his situation amidst the tragedies of the Midwest farm-belt, he added, "What we do not need here are 'justice advocates' or 'helping professionals' or 'morale boosting cheerleaders,' but pastors who are committed to the ministry of Word and Sacrament, open to grace, who care about people, and who will stay around to make it happen."

The replacement of a sense of call by the growth of careerism and professionalism has, as it always does, led to an elitist spirit in the ordained minstry. "Pastors want to be served instead of to serve," added John Cochran. "They want to view the ministry as a profession among the other professions, with its own career trajectory for success, to do their offical functions, have people flock to see them because they do them, and are surprised when they don't." "I really don't have much in common with the elitists and liturgical chauvinists among my clergy brethren," added another pastor. Indeed, one has to admit that, for all the good that the liturgical renewal movement has done to enhance the church's worship life in the last generation, when liturgical expertise is coupled with notions of professionalism it leads to an elitism in which liturgy becomes the clergy's special, peculiar technology in a world filled with technologies. Pastors hide behind it as their badge of uniqueness. What is really at work here is the desire, much like children who show off their toys to gain acceptance, to command respect and to gain vindication in the eyes of the world. St. Paul had a better solution: "Whoever boasts, let him boast of the Lord. . . . For it is not the man who commends himself that is accepted, but the man whom the Lord commends" (1 Cor. 1:31; 2 Cor. 10:18). God's call to ministry is sufficient and all the vindication we need.

I agree with Pastor Schmalenberger that the church as a whole, and clergy in particular, need to be renewed in the sense of the divine call as the motive for ministry. Fundamentally, the ordained ministry is not a profession; it is a calling. Different values are at work. The values and priorities of a career are simply incompatible with those of a *vocatio,* calling. "Seeing your life as under a call from God, and being willing to lay your life down for the sake of the community you serve," as Pastor Cochran described it, is a far cry from the life of the professional, whose private life is separated from the hours she "puts in" on the job. Servicing a clientele of individuals whose lives are separate from his own is a far cry from serving a community to whose life his own life is bound. Measuring the impact of a move or promotion on the basis of its effect on her career path and aims is a far cry from evaluating its effect on the community she serves. As Lyle Schaller, noted observer on church life, has commented,

> Cultural forces have been at work to turn vocations into careers. The transformation has been marked by a growing emphasis on credentials, by the emergence of career development centers, by

evaluating the week in terms of the hours worked rather than by the amount of good that was accomplished. . . . Careerism tends to still the prophetic voices of the teacher, the preacher, the army officer, the physician, the missionary and the nurse. Careerism encourages a change from service to self-interest. The rights, privileges, and perquisites of office become more important than duty, obligation and service. Loyalty to one's superiors replaces loyalty to the cause. Image is seen as more important than performance.[13]

Viewing the ministry as a career with its own privileges and trajectories for success robs pastors of their effectiveness in ministry. The laity are not dumb. They seek pastors who are committed to their calling, and they know when a pastor is out for the bucks and looking for prestige. Not a few times in the course of interviews was this mentioned as a major disappointment of laity in the clergy today. More than this, immeasurable damage has been done to the morale and self-esteem of congregations which have witnessed a succession of first-call pastors who stay three-to-five years and then move on to "bigger and better things." During the Vietnam era, when service in a combat zone was a feather in one's cap, this was called "getting your ticket punched." It may serve the career plans of the person, but it is absolutely deadly to congregations. What happens to the parish that is seen and sees itself as a "first-call" church, a stepping-stone for careers in ministry? First, as is common wisdom, most effective ministry does not begin until the fourth year. It takes several years to accumulate trust and knowledge of each other which lays a solid foundation for fruitful ministry together. Yet, the short-call pastor leaves before or just as this begins to happen. This in turn fosters a self-image among the members that they are a less-desirable parish for pastors, and that they are fated to a future filled with first-call pastors who will only serve them as long as they need to before they can move to better things. Not only does this negative self-image convince them they will not grow, it builds their resistance to change, because they know the pastor who proposes doing something new is not going to stay around long enough to bear the consequences of the proposed change. He is only doing it to enhance his prestige in the eyes of the "superiors" in the hierarchy. The congregation then gets a reputation as recalcitrant and stubborn, which in turn feeds the cycle of first-call, short-term pastorates.

In my third year of ministry at my first parish I put in a request to my bishop for a move to a parish "more to my liking." His answer, couched in very polite, diplomatic, subtle language was,

"Don't call me, I'll call you." It was the best thing a bishop has ever said to me. It freed me from the anxiety of where I was going to go next. For better or worse, I was stuck where I was, and I was freed me to devote my entire energy to serving St. Mark's-Temple, which I did with renewed relish. It was a turning point in my ministry there. A year later, when I was asked and interviewed for another call, I turned it down. I had discovered my real call was where I was. Together, that congregation and I went on to enjoy four more years of a very lively, exciting ministry. What would have been a shallow four-year apprenticeship became a healthy, effective eight-year ministry.

I use my case as an illustration of something many pastors in this study observed as a critical necessity in pastoral leadership: The need to stick around long enough to be effective. Though congregations, pastors, bishops and synods alike ignore or refuse to take the actions necessary to insure that it happens, it is common wisdom that effective pastoral ministry is tied to the length of one's pastorate. One must stay long enough to introduce strategic differences in ministry and to make sure that the changes stick. Only in doing so can a pastor develop the trust and commitment among members which will result in long-term growth in ministry, to say nothing of numbers. One simply has to say "No!" to the voices of careerism which beckon a pastor to greener pastures. "The real impact of my ministry was not felt until after my first six years," said Pastor Larry Smoose, "made possible because I deliberately avoided looking at other calls." The same should be said for associate pastors. Too often, said Pastor Rudowski, "associates move around the third or fourth year, which is just when they are able to make the greatest impact." Added Pastor Myron Herzberg, "I know of ministers in my synod who have been ordained twenty years, but still haven't the foggiest notion of what parish ministry is all about, nor experienced its joys, because they haven't stayed long enough in any parish to learn it." If the call to serve a parish means laying down one's life in service to that community, it is obvious that excellence in ministry means more than a "one-night stand." True faithfulness, be it in marriage or in ministry, occurs through the joys and sufferings of life together, not just the good times of the honeymoon period.

The issue of careerism, aided and abetted by the sin of ambition, is critical in the church's life today. In his book *Freedom For Ministry,* Richard Neuhaus suggests these two guidelines when dealing with issues related to one's call to ministry:

A good general rule by which to test our singleness of heart is that, when faced with choices, we give greater weight to the one that will require greater sacrifice. And another general rule: Choose the one that others would be less likely to choose.... They carried a protesting Ambrose to the church in order to make him a bishop. The corruption of the present-day church would be greatly reduced were more of its leaders compelled to office by obedience rather than attracted to office by ambition.[14]

And I would add another: Be prepared to have your plans interrupted, be ready to change the direction you planned or hoped to go to serve in a place or way you never counted on.

How pastors today face and answer the issue of careerism will determine their effectiveness in ministry and the vitality, even survival, of many of today's congregations. Churches are desperately seeking a pastor to love and serve them, who regards the parish ministry of Word and Sacrament as the most important work in the world, and who sees her parish as the congregation on which the whole success or failure of Christendom depends.

Coupled with this strong sense of divine call to ministry must be a lively personal faith. This, too, was cited by pastors and laity as a key element in pastoral leadership. And, as timeworn as the word is, there is no getting around the issue of sincerity. People expect the pastor to be a sincere person of faith who leads a godly life in and out of the pulpit, who is unashamed of Christianity, the church and the ministry in every situation. "People want a leader, someone committed to the Lord," commented Pastor Greg Wenhold. This commitment to the Lord was seen in a number of ways. Several people commented on the pastor's need for a personal devotional life. All of them indicated in their responses that time—usually two or more hours a week—was spent just on this. It was revealed in the way a pastor availed herself of the means of grace as a source for renewal and guidance. This does not mean, however, that pastors must maintain an image of being spiritually impregnable, as though they instead of God are the church's one foundation, a mighty fortress and a bulwark never failing. "A pastor has to allow the parish to minister to him. We don't do ourselves any favors by putting on airs of being spiritual superstars who are always in control and never show our need for grace and the care of others," said David Gleason. When I asked a member of a church in Philadelphia why their white pastor was so successful ministering in a black church, the person replied, "He was not afraid to share his pain and hurts with us. That is something black people can relate to."

A final issue on this matter of personal credibility and sincerity has to do with a controversial and painful issue at this time in the church. The issue must be addressed here, because numerous pastors and laity mentioned it as a major negative factor destroying clergy credibility in congregations today. The issue is divorce in the clergy ranks. Once a matter which automatically, either by the pastor himself or his bishop, removed the minister from his parish and even the active ordained ministry altogether, today's situation finds clergy divorces keeping pace with the rest of the society. At this writing one Lutheran seminary has five faculty and staff members going through divorces. In his years of serving in positions which brought him into contact with many bishops in the church, Pastor Cochran reported the numerous complaints about the high rate of divorce among the clergy and the resulting damage it does to congregations. In discussing the topic with some of my laypersons, one said, "Divorce always destroys, or at least damages, the respect people have for a pastor and the credibility of the office of ministry— regardless of the question of innocence or guilt on the part of the minister."

Yet, as serious as the issue is, both for the couples involved and for the damage clerical divorces do to congregations, often ministers are unwilling or incapable of coming to grips with the problem. It is a failure to take the Bible seriously on this issue (odd for clergy, who are called to be teachers of it), to distinguish Law and Gospel, and to acknowledge that there is a double-standard at work here. We fail to acknowledge that the New Testament teachings on divorce, especially those of Jesus (which current scholarship credits as being genuinely his and not the creation of the early church), are strongly opposed to divorce, either altogether or except in matters of adultery. We fail to recognize that what is at stake in clergy who divorce is not their salvation, but their qualification and credibility to exercise the office of ministry. The forgiveness of sins and justification by faith does not exempt us from doing all such good works as God has commanded and doing them for God's sake and not placing our trust in them as if thereby to merit favor (i.e., obtain salvation) before God. (If this section sounds like the language of the Augsburg Confession, Article VI, it is.)

We likewise fail to recognize that in this matter there is a double standard that has been in effect ever since the church was asked to select people of sound life and teaching to be authoritative preachers and teachers of the faith—and even the most cursory reading of the pastoral epistles (1 & 2 Timothy and Titus) witnesses to this. The double standard is simply this: What is expected of those who believe the Gospel is required of those called to proclaim it—again, not that those expectations are requirements for salvation on the part of the ordained, but for the sake of the community, the ordained are called to serve, to lay down their lives for them.

Instead of coming to grips with these truths, the best we can seem to do is wring our hands over the whole matter and cry, "Ain't it awful, something ought to be done"—but never quite getting around to doing much. Instead, believing that the Gospel of grace in Christ justifies us before God apart from what we do, we believe that we are freed from the judgment of others in this life as well. We forget the tension of Luther's understanding of Christian freedom: Though we stand before God free and justified for Jesus' sake, before our fellow humans we are bound as servants. What has taken its place has been the moral relativism and focus on self-fulfillment of our time. So, the call of ordination is superseded by the lure of personal fulfillment through career success. So the call to lifelong faithfulness in marriage takes a back seat to one's individual needs and wants. So church discipline is based on what everybody else is doing and the need for "understanding" of the complexities and varieties of divorce situations. All the while the laity look for shepherds who can lead and guide them, whose lives give evidence of being led by the Holy Spirit through persistent encounter with God's Word, and whose actions will not become, instead of the word of the cross (1 Cor. 1:18-23), the reason people do not believe the Gospel.

At the very least I suggest these general guidelines. First, as preventive medicine, we need education beginning at the seminary level and in later years through synodical retreats for both pastors and their spouses to reflect and grow in their understanding of the dual call to ministry and to marriage. Second, there needs to be a more consistent procedure on the part of the church in responding to situations where clerical marriages break down. Too often, as one bishop indicated to me, the problem is ignored, hoping it will go away of its own accord. Or action by the bishop's office comes too late in the process and serves only as damage control instead of helpful guidance for clergy couples and their parishes. When a minister's marriage reaches the point of breakdown, there should be a consistent procedure by which a pastor reports to the bishop's office (one would hope for a situation in which a bishop is in touch with his or her pastors well enough so that when this occurs it is not a surprise). Once the bishop's office knows of the existing problems, he should exercise flexibility in responding, depending on his assessment of the situation. In cases of marital separation, a response might be to grant a pastor a paid leave of absence from the parish to work out difficulties with a spouse. Where the marriage has reached the point of divorce, assessment needs to be made of the pastor continuing in his present call. Certainly the pastor should offer to resign. Again, flexibility in response seems in order, depending on the bishop's judgment of the situation, the circumstances of the divorce, and the congregation's interests. Actions may range from a leave of absence to resignation from the call, suspension from service in the parish for a period of time to continuation in the ministry under a vow of celibacy, to removal from the ordained ministry. In all events, it needs to be understood and practiced that the last word in the administration of ecclesiastical discipline in these matters rests with the bishop, not the private interests of the congregation or its pastor.

These actions should not be construed as punitive or legalistic, but made in light of the circumstances of the divorce and out of concern for the pastor and his or her family, the congregation, and the credibility of the office of ministry. The last issue cannot be ignored if we are to be committed to excellence in ministry. Whether we like it or not, the pastor is expected to "be different," to be "above reproach" (1 Timothy 3:2). Care must be taken that the pastoral office not be degraded by conduct which creates scandal. In his book, *Breach of Faith,* Theodore White argued that President Nixon's worst crime in Watergate was betraying the trust and confidence of the American people that the President is above the ugliness of politics, that he acts in the country's best interests and not his own, that he upholds the laws which express what America stands for, not breaks them.[15] The office of ministry is, also, an office whose credibility is based on trust in the person called to occupy it. The message of the person who is called to the office of ministry—the Gospel of grace and forgiveness through Jesus Christ—loses believeability when the marriage life of the one who preaches the Gospel is a living denial of its power to shape and guide lives and effect forgiveness in human relationships. In most cases, excellence in ministry goes down the drain. The laity know it, even if we will not admit it.

The above discussion has been lengthy (as it should be), but not meant to cast a shadow of gloom on the state of the clergy today—though what is dragging pastors down needs to be honestly faced. There are still many pastors doing good work in ministry and whose marriages are not falling apart. As we have seen these pastors exemplify excellence in ministry—an excellence born of a sense of their divine call to ministry, an ability to create and articulate a vision for their parish of what community in Christ is all about, and a persistence and enthusiasm to work for its realization. Their lives bear witness to the truth of the Gospel. Their excellence in pastoral leadership provides an indispensible foundation for overall excellence in ministry in the church.

CHAPTER IV

The Foundations of Excellence: Commitment, Ownership, and Leadership

"Will the people open themselves to what Christ gives his church: The Word and Sacraments?"—Rev. David Gleason, Palmyra, Pennsylvania

"Are members seen as gifts, and trusted for their gifts?"—Rev. Richard Bieber, Detroit, Michigan

"What is the energy level of people to put into the life of the church, to do the tasks of ministry?"—Rev. Richard Dowhower, Camp Hill, Pennsylvania

"They [the Church Council] must be open ... and be willing to allow for new ideas, for growth, to listen to the pastor, the staff, and members and discern the best direction."—Pat Smith, Volunteer Coordinator, God's Love Lutheran Church, Newtown, Pennsylvania.

These statements, taken together, point to what lies at the heart of issues relating to achieving excellence in the ministry of the laity. Openness to the Gospel, ownership and leadership of the congregation's program of ministry and the commitment of time and energy: These were the observations cited most often by pastors and laity in the congregations interviewed. Without these elements even the best of parish pastors will find the going rough. But, if one examines these elements closer, what is really involved here is, how do the members of the parish understand themselves as called by God to exercise the church's ministry of the Gospel? Just as the challenge to excellence in ministry begins for pastors with their understanding of God's call through their ordination to exercise the ministry of Word and Sacraments, the laity's (Greek: *laos,* "people") commitment to excellence in ministry begins with an understanding of being called by God in baptism. The priesthood of all believers means that all are given the whole mission of the church's ministry of the Gospel in the world.

So, the first question becomes the key starting point: "Will the people open themselves to what Christ gives his church: the Word and the Sacraments?" Or, as another pastor more bluntly put it, "After himself, a pastor's biggest problem is his congregation. Are they willing to be biblically faithful?"

It is a very simple question, yet the key, if a parish understands excellence in ministry to include faithfulness to the Gospel, not just having a slick religious organization. Yet, too often, out of a concern for survival or to "be like others"—i.e., successful—the integrity of our witness is sacrificed by both clergy and laity. "It is amazing to me," said Pastor Steinbruck, "what we do to obfuscate the Gospel." Like the religious leaders trying to discredit Jesus in John 9, we will go to great lengths to avoid dealing with the truth and pursuing simple faithfulness in our mission as God's people. The process reminds me of a story Tom Peters tells which he believes typifies what is going wrong in organizations today. An executive told Peters:

"Let me tell you about two meetings I sat in on. Both were with companies having some problems with quality control.

"One company was professionally managed. Their approach to the problem was to analyze everything. How many doors, say, were falling off? What percentage of the doors were falling off? How much would it cost to stick 'em back on? What were the chances of getting sued? How much advertising would it take to counteract the bad publicity?

"Not once did they actually talk about the doors, or the hinges, or why . . . they were falling off. They were not interested in solving the problem; they just wanted to manage the mess.

"The other meeting was at Coleman Stove. They were having a problem with some boilers that were cracking. So picture it: the Executive Committee assembles. There is the usual small talk: How are the kids? How is the golf game? Then the Service Department comes in with the reports, the clipboards, the yellow pencils, and everybody hunkers down for a serious discussion. Well, you know how long that meeting lasted? About thirty seconds. Old Man Coleman sits bolt upright in his chair and bellows out: 'You mean we've got goods out there that aren't working? Get 'em back. Replace 'em, and find out why. . . .' And that was the end of the meeting. There was no financial analysis.

There was no legal analysis. There was no customer relations analysis. There was no ... analysis. The issue was the integrity of the product—which meant there was no issue at all. We stand by it, and that's that."[1]

The lesson is this: When issues arise in a church, if pastors and laity would concentrate less on "managing the messes," less on what might happen if such-and-such an action were taken, and more on the integrity and biblical faithfulness of their mission, letting these criteria guide their decisions, much of what paralyzes parish ministry today would be cured. A Passage from Dietrich Bonhoeffer's _Life Together,_ written a half-century ago, addresses this issue with the same clarity and insight it did then:

> How, for example, will we ever attain certainty and confidence in our personal and church activity if we do not stand on solid biblical ground? It is not our heart that determines our course, but God's Word. But who in this day has any proper understanding of the need for scriptural proof? How often we hear innumerable arguments 'from life' and 'from experience' put forward as the basis for most crucial decisions, but the argument from Scripture is missing. And this authority would perhaps point in exactly the opposite direction.[2]

Again, as in the previous chapters, the key is focusing on and faithfully executing the basics of what the church is to be about in the world. The concrete shape this takes in practice is a shared ministry, rooted in baptism and ordination, between the members of a congregation and with their pastor.

Inasmuch as the congregation's exercise of its ministry is a shared effort between the laity and the pastor(s), a whole host of pastor-people issues present themselves, some of which relate back to concerns mentioned in the last chapter. One was a question raised by Pastor Dowhower: "What are the expectations among the laity of competence in their pastor?" Several other pastors also mentioned the need for the laity to expect competence in their pastor; if pastors perform poorly, it is because laity allow them to get away with it. They let pastors get away with making only a few house calls a month, with poorly prepared and delivered sermons, with failing to develop a program of worship, education and outreach ministry in the parish, with failing to maintain a program of continuing education.

The truth is, laypeople will get the kind of ministry they allow their pastors to give them. More than one pastor commented,

"There are some ministers in this synod who, were it not for the ministry, could not hold a job anywhere." That statement should bother all of us—laity, parish pastors, bishops and seminary faculties. Is the parish ministry becoming a welfare system for those who cannot make it elsewhere? The church—for the sake of the ministry which Christ has entrusted to his people—deserves better than that. There is much the laity can do to see that the church gets better than that.

Simply put, there is much the people can do to help their pastor strive for excellence in ministry. One pastor in this study commented on how he constantly sought evaluations and feedback from his members. This should not be, however, just the pastor's desire, but a way congregations give support to their pastors—through their prayers, honest dialogue with them on issues, advice, bearing of burdens and sorrows and forgiveness.

Such support should not fall only to a mutual ministry committee, though such groups are extremely helpful. It is a task for the whole people of God. Clergy need to know up front that their members pray for them (in my first nine years of ministry, only once did a member mention that she did this for me). One pastor in this study remarked how during an illness he was simply overwhelmed by the knowledge that people were spontaneously going to the church to pray for him. Other times when he was ministering to people in crisis parishioners would call him to ask how he was. Such simple knowledge can go very far in preventing or easing the common tensions which arise at times between pastors and parishioners. It can prevent the distancing between the pastor and the laity which sometimes happens. Dietrich Bonhoeffer's observation on this matter is quite to the point:

> This brings us to a point at which we hear the pulsing heart of all Christian life in unison. A Christian fellowship lives and exists by the intercession of its members for one another, or it collapses. I can no longer condemn or hate a brother for whom I pray, no matter how much trouble he is causing me. . . . There is no dislike, no personal tension, no estrangement that cannot be overcome by intercession as far as our side of it is concerned. Intercession is the purifying bath into which the individual and the fellowship must enter everyday.[3]

It is from such simple knowledge that pastors know and experience that members also forgive them of their sins, bear with their shortcomings and speak the truth in love to them when the situation warrants. When I was in seminary a good friend in the ministry told me, "When I look back on my first years in the parish and the dumb things I did, I thank God for the forbearance and forgiveness the people of that parish extended me." I did not quite understand how or why that could be so until I got into my first parish and proceeded to do my share of dumb things and experienced the same forbearance and forgiveness. To this day I recall how, at a very difficult time, my ministry in that parish was given a new start by a layperson (my council vice-president). Instead of standing aloof and criticizing me as quite a few people were doing, he had the courage to confront me candidly about the problems as he saw them and suggest how together we could surmount them.

Another issue which was raised in the last chapter was that of the longevity of a pastor's call. There is much that laity can do to nurture a climate which encourages a pastor to stay long enough to do an effective ministry.

Undoubtedly for many this will immediately raise the sensitive, sometimes divisive, issue of clerical compensation. Not a few pastors in this study raised this as an important issue for congregations, and the church as a whole. One pastor said that he knew some clergy are "out for the buck," but he also believes not a few congregations are "just plain cheap" when it comes to the financial care of their pastor. I myself have known of cases where ministers could have (though did not) receive food stamps at their compensation level.

"Let the elders who rule well be considered worthy of double honor (literally, in Greek, *times,* 'compensation'), especially those who labor in preaching and teaching; for the Scripture says, '. . . the laborer deserves his wages'" (1 Tim. 5:17). The pastor's compensation belongs as the first and most important order of business come budget preparation time. Congregations do not, in the long run, save themselves anything by attempting to save in this area.

But, even where congregations find that, because of their size and situation, the price they can pay for a pastor plateaus, there are other ways of caring for their pastor. A simple question to ask is, "How do you say, 'Thanks'?" Many companies have "end of the year" bonuses; why shouldn't churches? Such gifts could be accorded on the occasion of anniversaries of ordination, Christmas, anniversaries of call, etc. One pastor mentioned how on one such anniversary his congregation provided him a trip to Germany. Another pastor recalled with thankfulness how he had been overwhelmed by the Christmas gift his little church of 45 average Sunday attendance had given him after one year of ministry. It exceeded substantially the amount he had received at a former church of greater size where he had served longer.

I don't mean to suggest that money is the only way a congregation can say thanks or care for their pastor in a way which encourages her to stay. Most businesses have regular times at which they
recognize performance by individuals. Why not a pastor? Another
option would be including in the agreement between a pastor and
a congregation opportunities for the pastor to pursue other interests in the ministry (extra continuing education programs, military
chaplaincy, synodical service, writing books). This might be especially fruitful for smaller parishes which cannot pay as well as other
parishes, but by their smaller size can allow the pastor more free
time to pursue other interests. Whatever the method, in almost all
cases congregations that take care of their pastors will find themselves justly rewarded. Most ministers are very dedicated to their
calling, are very generous with their income (clergy donate on average about eight percent of their income to the church; the national
average on charitable giving is about three percent), and, if they
feel they are being treated in a fair and caring manner, are more
than willing to work for less money than their peers who choose
other professions.

Just as members of a parish exercise their church's ministry of
the Gospel in partnership with their pastor, they also work with
each other to fulfill their church's mission. This, too, raises a number of issues which merit consideration. "How much time and energy do people have to devote to doing the tasks of ministry?"
asked Pastor Dowhower. Time pressure was cited by a number of
respondents as a critical issue facing the church today. "And I do
not buy the 'too busy' argument from people," said Greg Wenhold.
"It precludes the work of the Holy Spirit; it is an excuse, an analysis,
not an answer." Indeed, parishes that exhibit excellence in ministry
do not accept the old saw that people do not have time to attend to
the church's work in the world and to building up the Body of
Christ. Certainly nowhere is the time crunch more consistently felt
and raised than in suburbia. Yet time and again I found people of
lively faith and practice devoting themselves to the work of their
parish in a manner which excelled over others. I listened in awe to
Pastor Gleason describe how more than ten lay leaders in his parish
in Hershey, Pennsylvania, had organized and led the morning and
evening prayer offices *daily,* attended on average by from 15 to 20
people at each service. Or consider Good Shepherd Church in Cincinnati: Whereas the average congregation in America has about 30
percent of its baptized membership in Sunday worship (and those
above this average are weighted disproportionately in favor of small,
rural parishes), Good Shepherd averages over 50 percent of its bap-

tized membership in church on Sunday. Committed laity do make
time for their church.

This points to a critical issue for laity in achieving excellence in
their parish's ministry: Will they own—that is, take responsibility
and leadership for—their church's ministry? Where they do, amazing results happen. One of my three churches is a case in point. At
the beginning of the 1980s Christ, Aspers, was almost given up for
dead. Worship attendance was averaging in the 30s. The membership was mostly over 50 years old. The building was badly in need
of repair. Today nobody is giving Christ, Aspers, up for dead. More
and more the question is, "How far can we go?" The building has
been renovated, with more in the planning. Attendance has doubled. The Sunday School is renewed and innovatively growing.
Quite honestly, all this has occurred with less-than-normal clergy involvement in the life of the congregation, since Christ Church
shares its pastor with two other churches. What has happened over
the last several years has been the result of the commitment and
vision of the laity. As one member describes it, the people decided
their church was going to survive and they set about doing it.

According to Richard Bieber, our congregations need to recover
the fullest sense of our Lutheran understanding of the priesthood of
all believers. This means more than just getting everyone to do a
job or fill a committee position. It means members ministering to
one another, caring for and nurturing each other in the faith.[4]

"Welcome one another, as Christ has welcomed you, for the
glory of God" (Romans 15:7). The care and nurture of members begins the moment a visitor comes through the door of the church. Is
this person welcomed with the same warmth as a fellow member of
the Body of Christ? Is she visibly noticed and made to feel at home
by the members? Are visitors to the church in turn visited by the
pastor and members shortly after they have been to the church? Peter Rudowski always insisted on visiting newcomers within forty-
eight hours after they had been to a service. Any visit later than that
will be perceived by people as indifference on the part of the pastor and the congregation, as something they "finally got around to
doing." Sadly, people described cases of visiting a church repeatedly
and not being greeted by people in the congregation, not assisted
with the service if they were new to the Lutheran Church, and not
visited by the pastor or the people until their third or fourth visit, if
at all.

Contrast this to the kind welcome Pastor Schwanenberg of
MacArthur Park Lutheran Church in San Antonio said visitors to his
church receive: "No one gets out of here without at least five hand-

shakes and a hug." During my internship at Good Shepherd in Cincinnati, I witnessed members dropping by a visitor's home on the same day he or she had attended the church. A pastor followed up by visiting on Monday or Tuesday. It has been my observation that congregations which are perceived as friendly and receptive to newcomers usually have one or two people who are the unappointed, unofficial "welcomers of strangers." These people take it upon themselves to watch for guests who come to the church—to welcome them, get them to sign the guest register, and then make sure the pastor gets introduced to them.[5]

Some, of course, will look upon this as a trivial matter. But I think many pastors would agree that congregations drop the ball in reaching out to new people precisely because they overlook such "trivialities." We should not forget our Lord's admonition to remember the strangers:

> "And the righteous will answer, 'Lord . . . when did we see thee a stranger and welcome thee?' And the King will answer them, 'Truly I say to you, even as you did it to the least of these my brethren, you did it also to me'" (Matt. 25:38-40).

How we welcome people to our congregations says much about our witness and service to our Lord in subtle, even unnoticeable ways. In late 1986 I invited Pastor John Cochran to preach at our joint parish. He brought with him two young men from his neighborhood, one of whom was unbaptized because, being black, he did not know whether he could join an almost all-white denomination. He was not sure he could trust the members. John and his two traveling companions ate dinner with us the night before, spent the night in our home and attended services the next day. Pastor Cochran later reported to me that his friend had decided to be baptized. His experience of being welcomed in my parishes had broken down the barriers of suspicion. We had not been conscious of what was occurring in him during his visit, yet the simple act of welcoming had been a ministry to that young man that opened him to the Gospel. Our care and nurture of each other in the faith begins with the way we welcome those who come through our doors. This is one job laity cannot leave to the pastor. The most important relationships in a parish that wants long-term strength are not between the people and their pastor, but among themselves.

But caring for each other does not begin and end with welcoming newcomers. What happens to people after they join the church? Are they still welcomed, as Christ has welcomed his church, for the glory of God? Or, as happens in so many cases, do they walk in the front door and walk out the back door of inactivity six months later? In practical terms, there is a difference between being added to the rolls of a church and becoming a member of it. Caring and nurturing people in the faith means that laypeople take responsibility for each other. This can happen in a variety of ways: Simply praying for one another; bearing one another's burdens, or what Myron Herzberg described in his rural Iowa congregation as a "sharing of sufferings empowered by the Gospel;" and training and developing one another in the work of the church. David Houck, a member of one of my congregations and a very active layperson in our synod, said his dedication to service in the church had been the result of the encouragement and training he had received from a fellow member. At God's Love Lutheran Church in Newtown, Pennsylvania, member Pat Smith is the "Volunteer Coordinator," a position in which she works along with a shepherding program to guide, encourage, and develop people in ministry.

In his short but to-the-point book on Christian community, *Life Together,* Bonhoeffer describes the various types of ministry which occur in a Christian community:

The Ministry of Holding One's Tongue [First!]
The Ministry of Meekness
The Ministry of Listening
The Ministry of Helpfulness
The Ministry of Bearing
The Ministry of Proclaiming
The Ministry of Authority.[6]

There's no better delineation of the ways in which Christians nurture and care for one another in Christian community. Bonhoeffer's description applies to the work of the whole Christian community, not just the pastors (though comments on pastoral practice abound in the book). Ministry in a church cannot be "left to the pros." It is the work of every baptized believer.

At the heart of this, of course, is the need for leaders among the laity who are committed to the congregation's growth in ministry. And where the rubber hits the road in this regard is with the Church Council (Board, Vestry, Session, etc.). Will the Council be made up of, in the words of Pastor Bob Holley, "trustworthy leaders with a vision and willingness to serve?" Will they set the tone and the priorities for ministry? Will they be, as the opening statement of this chapter mentioned, the people who listen to the pastor, the staff, the members, and with an openness to new ideas and growth, discern the best way for the congregation? Will the Council serve the function for which Acts 6 indicates such leaders were appointed, which is to free the pastor to do his or her unique work of preaching, teaching, presiding at worship and giving pastoral care for people? (It is important to note here the case of Stephen who was appointed to care for the temporal affairs of the church but also became a public Christian witness.) Will they have the courage to address and make decisions on issues facing the parish? Will they expect competence among themselves and the other lay leaders of the parish?

One pastor told how his Church Council *fired* two lay leaders for not doing their jobs. "This is the only church I know that fires its volunteers," he remarked. "Did the two leave the church?" I asked. His reply was no. The people had high expectations of one another to do good work for the church and understood that decisions are made in terms of what best served the church's ministry, and not on the basis of personalities. At Trinity Lutheran Church in Lancaster, Pastors Lehman and Hoffman observed:

> "One of our great strengths has always been our vestry. We have had a tradition of strong vestry leadership. We expect it of them; each person is expected to worship regularly, be an evangelist, participate in our educational programs, grow in stewardship, and exhibit the ability to make objective decisions on the basis of God's Word, not 'who did you last talk to'."[7]

"When the Council gets behind an idea, it will come about," said one respondent. Exactly. It cannot be denied or understressed that lay leadership, especially in the Church Council, can make or break a congregation's growth in ministry. Just how much difference the actions of a Council can make is illustrated by this story from my years as a pastor at St. Mark's-Temple in Clifton Heights, Pennsylvania. In 1978 a new hymnal was introduced in Lutheran churches. Few events in a parish are more difficult or can cause as much dissension as a change to a new hymnal. (The problem is not unique to this century. Even the Book of Common Prayer had difficulty winning acceptance in the 17th-century Anglican Church.) While I was strongly in favor of the new hymnal's adoption, the Council never could bring itself to decide for or against it. They believed the congregation ought to see it and decide for itself. The lack of key lay leadership to point the way for the members, combined with other factors at work in the parish at that time, enabled groups opposed to the hymnal to command attention. The result was a resounding negative vote on the hymnal in June of 1980. Five years later the idea of switching to the now not-so-new hymnal was reintroduced. This time the Council took charge of the program, told the congregation what they wanted to see happen and set the time-table for its accomplishment. The result? The hymnal was oversubscribed in four months and learned in less than one. The lay leadership made the critical difference between failure on one occasion and success five years later.

Involved here is another equally important factor, yet an area in which many congregations fall flat on their faces: sharing the decision-making processes in the parish. Too often one hears the comment, "Of course, we are open and want to see new members join our church." Yet in reality new members often are seen as a way to recreate yesterday's congregation, yesterday's program, yesterday's activities, rather that as members of the Body of Christ with their own unique gifts and talents and vision of what their congregation can be. Pastor Rudowski put the issue bluntly: "Are the laity willing to pay the price for growth, which means caring enough for new members to allow them to share in shaping and directing the future ministry of the congregation? Growth means change." That brings us back to the question posed earlier: Will the laity be committed to their congregation's growth in ministry?

Embedded in the last story is a critical issue for pastors as well. Will the pastor seek out and trust the laity for their gifts and leadership? In healthy churches, the laity are trusted for and given opportunities to express the gifts God has given them to do ministry—not, as one pastor commented, "regarded as dumb sheep" which always have to be told what to do, how to do it, and constantly monitored to see that they are not messing up. Again I recall those laypeople at Palm Lutheran Church in Hershey, Pennsylvania, who run the daily offices of morning and evening prayer. One of them is an eleven-year-old boy. One Texan pastor's maxim on this matter goes straight to the point: "I try to stay out of the way of lay-run ministries." So should every pastor. Pastor Stephen Youngdahl in Austin, Texas, has a simple method for accomplishing this: All committees meet on the same Tuesday night of every month (which also insures a greater division of labor among the laity), and he and his staff visit every one of them in that evening. This forces the laity, especially the committee chairpersons, to take responsibility for their own programs. They can't "leave it up to the pros." If the laity doesn't do it, it doesn't get done. The pastors are responsible to, but not for, a committee. They assist where needed or called upon, and see to it that the congregation's program of ministry is faithful to the biblical and confessional tradition. But they don't do the work the laity ought to do.

In my eight years of ministry at St. Mark's Temple, I rarely attended a finance or property meeting. It was the members' job to take care of the bricks and bucks. This does not mean I was uninvolved with or ignorant of what they were doing. I met regularly with the chairpeople to go over concerns. I focused my attention on the "people" committees—such as Christian Education, Worship, Social Ministry. Yet with the exception of the Worship Committee I rarely attended a full meeting. Indeed, at one point the Christian Education Committee chairperson had the wise audacity to say to me, "If you are going to meet with me beforehand to talk about what my committee is doing and planning, don't show up at the meeting also. We can take care of ourselves. Go visit somebody and take care of them, and if we need you we'll call you." That committee was one of the most productive we had. Pastors ought to pray for, have the wisdom to recognize and the humbleness to listen to quality lay leaders such as that person.

In *Passion For Excellence* Peters quotes a statement by Bill Gore: "We can't run the business. We learned over twenty-five years ago to let the business run itself. Commitment, not authority, produces results."[8] When I ran that statement by one of the pastors in this study, he nodded his head in agreement. Theologically it is so: Our understanding of the priesthood of all believers to which we are called in baptism makes the front line of Christian ministry in the world the work of the laity. It is their witness to Christ. Pastors need to make sure the church's mission of teaching and preaching the Gospel stays on track. But it is the laity who are the main force in carrying out Christian witness in the world day to day and building up the Body of Christ. When pastors recognize this, trust the laity for the gifts they bring to do ministry in their parish, serve them by seeking ways to help them do their work and then get out of their way so they can do it, lo and behold things get done. Good things happen. The few stories mentioned here, repeated in congregations across the church, bear witness to it. The laity, just as much as the pastor, are critical to a congregation's pursuit of excellence in ministry.

CHAPTER V

Expressions of Excellence

Mission, pastoral leadership, lay commitment: these are the basic
foundations of excellence in parish ministry. They are concretely
expressed in activities which are the basic work of the community
of faith: worship, education, and care and outreach. In strong
churches these activities are marked by a commitment to quality
and united by one purpose: to get the Gospel communicated, so
that believers might be strengthened in their faith and unbelievers
brought to faith in Jesus as their Lord and Saviour.

QUALITY WORSHIP. In the Augsburg Confession, "ministry" is described as the office of Word and Sacrament. The church is that as-
sembly of believers in which the Word is preached purely and the
Sacraments administered according to the Gospel (AC V, VII). The
experience of pastors and laity in this study repeatedly bore out
what our theology affirms: Worship is the heart and soul, the center
and strength of a congregation. Many pastors said that establishing
quality, lively worship had been their first order of business upon
beginning their ministry with a congregation. The adjectives *quality*
and *lively* cannot be overlooked if a parish commits itself to excellence in its ministry.

As the saying goes, "There is no substitute for quality." When
Pastor Siefken came to the troubled and debt-ridden congregation
of Prince of Glory in Madison Heights, Michigan, in 1970, his initial
concerns were simply "trying to do good worship, to make it the
best it could be." That meant "that those who lead worship must
have prepared themselves thoroughly and that those who worship,
including the leaders, must be prepared fully to participate." Quality
worship requires training and education at all levels of the congregation. It is, as the word liturgy—*leitourgia*—originally was used to
mean, "the work of the people." As such, it can be done either well,
with proper care and attention, or poorly and slovenly.

Excellence in worship begins, of course, with the pastor. Robert
Benne, professor at Roanoke College and noted lay theologian, reaf-

firms the importance of pastors giving attention to and planning for what occurs in the worship life of the parish. In the churches I surveyed, liturgical styles and abilities varied from pastor to pastor, and services ranged from a "high" to a "low" church liturgy, but in each case all things were done well and in an exciting, interesting manner. Such was also the case with the preaching. "There simply is no substitute for good, well-done preaching," commented a pastor. Added a layperson: "It is important that the pastor be well read, that he knows what is going on in the world and relates the Gospel to people's lives when he preaches." A survey of time taken in sermon preparation bore out these pastors' commitment to quality in worship and preaching—they spent an average of 11-12 hours a week in preparing and doing worship, including preaching. One pastor gave an entire day each week to preparing the Sunday sermon. That's a far cry from how one pastor described the way a supervisory pastor he worked with in seminary prepared his sermons: He had the seminarian read the lessons for the week to him as they vested for the service.

Quality worship is lively worship, not just in the sense that the liturgy and preaching are "executed" well, but in the ample opportunities the service offers members to be a community of prayer which in turn strengthens and nourishes them in the faith. This liveliness repeatedly evidenced itself in two ways. One was in the variety and frequency of worship services offered in local parishes. Worship was not just a Sunday-morning affair. Holy Spirit Church in West Bloomfield, Michigan, holds a Saturday evening service. Weekday Eucharists were often reported, e.g., St. John's Lutheran Church, Winters, Texas, and St. John's Church, Fairfield, Pennsylvania. As mentioned in the last chapter, one suburban congregation in Palmyra, Pennsylvania, has daily morning and evening prayer led completely by the laity. Said the pastor, Dave Gleason, "I trained the people in the history and performance of these prayer offices, and they've just run with the program ever since. . . . It is probably the best evangelism work we do in our area, just listing on the sign in front of our church, 'Daily Prayer—9:00 a.m. and 7:00 p.m., Monday through Friday'."

The second mark of liveliness in worship was in the appreciation and use of the liturgical calendar in the worship life of the parish. Capturing the diverse themes, moods and experience of the Christian faith insures that the liturgy will always be fresh and new, not the "same old, same old" week-in, week-out routine. "We have our liturgical tradition as a beautiful gift to bring to every congregation, every community," commented Pastor Cochran. We too often neglect this gift. The richness and diversity of the church year is a boost for faith. It is interesting to note how Dietrich Bonhoeffer, during his years of imprisonment by the Nazis, marked time not by the calendar year, but by the church year.[1] It was a reminder that God, not humankind, rules over history and that the time of his life was ultimately in God's hands alone. Churches with a lively worship life invariably take advantage of the opportunities the liturgical calendar affords to tell the story of Jesus for the edification of the faithful.

The last and most important factor: The worship was intentionally, distinctly and unapologetically Lutheran in its focus. That is, it stood within the catholic tradition of the liturgy and focused on the centrality of Word and Sacrament for the congregation's life. "It is the root of our identity, how God calls and renews us," commented Pastor Mark Radecke. It defines what the church is to be about. Recent years have seen an increasing emphasis on the congregation's "programmatic" ministry. The parish is seen as a place where all manner of programs, mostly social ministry in nature, take place. While these all may be important things a congregation does, Pastor Tim Ohlmann warned, "They can't become the tail that wags the dog. Worship has to be central." Nor should what is done liturgically be decided on the basis of what will appeal to newcomers. In some churches such a focus has sacrificed liturgical fidelity for what will bring in more members. Large churches can be found in every denomination, regardless of the kind of liturgy which is followed. Growth in members has no relation to the kind of liturgy done, though how it is done matters much. In the end what matters most is being faithful to one's confessional tradition.

In sum, being consciously Lutheran defines what quality worship was all about. Wrote David Gleason some years ago:

> For doing the liturgy well is more than just a matter of having leaders who know what to do when, or who can stand and read and sit and sing with grace, clarity, dignity, beauty, and deliberateness. Good liturgy is a matter of clearly centering on Word and Sacraments in the life of faith, and of perceiving the whole liturgical event as that which points to the center.[2]

How is such a full and high-quality worship life developed in these congregations? Growth in ministry did not occur all at once. Several key elements helped congregations achieve growth in the quality of a parish's worship life. Education was one: "We tried all we could do to help people to learn the liturgy," said Rev. Bob Holley. He said it was preached about, taught in classes, written in newsletters and practiced in training events before services or dur-

ing other specially scheduled times. Changes were often done on a
trial basis. "At Dale City, we had weekly Communion on a six-month
trial basis," Holley continued. "People voted at the end of the six
months whether they wanted to continue with the new practice or
return to the old. After six months, no one voted no." This points to
another factor: Lay ownership of the process of change. "The pastor
has to lead, not force, change," said one layperson. The pastor has a
clear responsibility to teach and inform the congregation about the
church's teaching and practice on worship and raise the issues for
her people to consider. But successful liturgical change occurs only
where the laity, especially the leadership, are committed to and responsible for carrying out the changes that are made. "I preached
and taught about the centrality of the Eucharist for our faith," commented Myron Herzberg, "and waited until the day came when the
people asked me how we could improve our practice in this area."

Extremely negative in this regard are two tendencies which have
been at work in recent years. Too often liturgical reforms have
come across as "ordered from on high" (i.e., the national church).
"I like you, Pastor," said a sweet, elderly lady as I greeted people in
the narthex following a congregational meeting in which the people
had overwhelmingly voted down a new hymnal change, "but I know
synod is not going to like us for this!"

The other negative is forced change by pastoral fiat or manipula-
tion in which people's traditions, piety and way of worshipping
come to be perceived as not only wrong, but invalid. Such disres-
pect accomplishes nothing but rebellion or grudging compliance.
Wrote Leigh Jordahl, religion professor at Luther College in De-
corah, Iowa:

> We are, none of us, going to get any place with renewal of any
> kind unless we build respectfully on the already existing piety of
> our parishes.[3]

Effective liturgical reform is highly connected to the degree of
trust people have in their pastor. They must believe that he or she
is acting in the best interests of the parish. Such trust is often related to how long a pastor has been at a parish. Frequently pastors
in this study mentioned how major changes did not occur until several years after they had been in their parishes. "I waited until I had
established a certain degree of trust and credibility in the church,"
said one pastor, "and when the people came and asked me what I
would like to see happen in the church to improve its ministry, I
said, 'Don't let me go on any longer being a part of my congrega-

tion's spiritual malnutrition. Permit me to do the work I was ordained to do and have the Eucharist every Sunday.'"

In sum, where liturgical reform is undertaken patiently, with
care and openness, with great education and lay ownership of the
process of change, and as an opportunity to improve the congregation's faithful exercise of its ministry, there one finds quality worship enjoyed by all.

QUALITY EDUCATION was the second key expression of excellence
in ministry. These pastors and congregations placed a high pre-
mium on education, both in terms of the pastor's continuing education and the educational life of the parish. It was not unusual for
pastors to report that they spent more than ten hours a week on
teaching preparation and time in class.

Adult education ranked high in importance. In describing the
critical factors which contributed to his congregation's growth in
the last ten years, Pastor Steve Rode of Christ Lutheran Church, San
Antonio, wrote: "Our centerpiece over the past ten years has been
attention to Adult Bible Study." His comment underscored an observation of Pastor Neal Boese of Michigan: "Studies of churches which
have sustained growth over the last thirty years revealed one consistent factor in all of them: Quality adult education." This flies in
the face of what passes for common wisdom, that the key educational activity in a church ought to focus on the children, its "future
members" (which in these mobile times usually turns out not to be
the case). Pastor Boese responded to this "wisdom" with a wise observation of his own: "Jesus taught adults and played with children.
Our churches teach children and play with adults." "You may not
always have children in your church," a pastor said to my church
council a few years ago, "but you will always have adults. So, teach
them well."

At Messiah Lutheran Church in Detroit, adult Bible classes are
not only a key program for adult members, but for outreach as
well. Pastor Bieber reported that attendance at his classes is always
in excess of forty people, and that the classes draw people from all
walks of life inside and outside the parish.

Though adult education is of prime importance, in healthy
churches the drive to learn more about the Christian faith and its
implications for today permeates the entire organization. "I really
get on my people when they don't take advantage of the educational opportunities given them here at our church," commented
Pastor Siefken. "The thing I like about Lutheranism is that it requires you to think." The commitment to high-quality Christian education was marked by two characteristics. First, a strong commit-

ment to raise awareness in people as to what a Lutheran way of being Christian means. "I want my people to be more consciously Lutheran," described Richard Dowhower of his educational efforts. "I want them to be theologically sound, and not part of some general religious grouping." Being distinctly Lutheran does not mean being parochial. Indeed, Lutheranism's historically theological place in the church catholic has been that of a catalyst of dialogue as to what the whole Christian church ought to believe and teach. But, to do that means one must know and appreciate one's unique heritage, not simply accept it as one more expression in the vegetable soup which is religion in America today or even reject it by trying to be like everyone else. Wrote Peter Rudowski from Good Shepherd Church in Cincinnati:

> We do not try to be all things to all people. We freely admit our weaknesses and strengths, and try to build from strength. . . . We are a Lutheran congregation. We do not apologize for our roots. We are biblical. I believe people today want their churches to take firm stands. Both liberal and conservative churches can grow if they stand firmly on their beliefs. Jesus spits out those with a lukewarm faith (Rev. 3:16).

Pastor Tim Ohlmann, serving in a multi-racial and cultural area in North Philadelphia added, "It is important to clarify our identity to other Protestants and Roman Catholics alike and be honest about our differences." If mission means knowing who you are and what you are to be about, it can only happen where there is an appreciation and fidelity to one's biblical and confessional tradition.

The other notable quality in these churches was the tremendous and innovative variety of educational programs. Education meant more than just Sunday School. There was a wide variety of programs for all ages and levels of understanding. Denominational and non-denominational resources (e.g., Bethel Bible Series) were employed. One large congregation had developed a "school of religion" which included an innovative confirmation program. Instead of the often ineffective and tedious once-a-week confirmation classes, a pastor had compressed the program into six Saturday sessions of five hours (including lunch break) over two years. This enabled him to spend more time with the students and more thoroughly cover a given topic, in addition to providing a welcome relief to the heavy scheduling demands of the traditional format. Other pastors developed their own devotionals and pamphlets on various topics for distribution to the people (especially effective in multi-church parishes where the pastor, due to worship scheduling, is often cut off from participation in the Sunday School).

Variety, innovation, faithfulness to one's heritage, commitment to learning: These are the marks of a quality educational program which seeks to fulfill Jesus' commission to his church, "Go into all the world . . . teaching them to observe all I have commanded you" (Matthew 28:19-20). Without it mission—knowing who you are and what you are to be about—does not happen.

The last expression of excellence in ministry was in QUALITY CARE AND OUTREACH. We have touched on this topic in earlier chapters where we described the importance of the laity's care for one another. This section treats the theme at greater length and in greater detail. Simply put, in lively congregations the way people care for their own overflows and reaches out beyond its doors to bring the Gospel to its community and beyond.

The principle which describes effective care and outreach in the parish is the French lay theologian Jacques Ellul's statement: "Think globally—act locally."[4] Effective care and outreach is a local event, though its actions are always guided by the universal horizon of the Gospel.

In Center City Lutheran Parish (CCLP) of Philadelphia, "thinking globally—acting locally" is an article of faith known as neighborhood ministry. As mentioned in earlier chapters, pastors are required to live in the communities of the parishes they serve. Instead of chasing people who have moved to the suburbs, these congregations have re-rooted themselves into their neighborhood. John Cochran, coming to a dying white congregation in the heart of the black community of Southwerk, put this question to his members: "Will Emmanuel Lutheran's membership reflect the population of our neighborhood?" They did, and what was a dying congregation of 150 members now numbers 1,000. At another of the CCLP congregations, St. Simeon's, the pastor reported that two-thirds of their neighborhood had at some point been inside their building. Programs for people in CCLP abound: Summer day camps, a school of diaconal ministry, youth sports league, social services, a parochial school system which expanded a few years ago to include a high school program which I'm told places all its graduates in college, a food bank, and thrift stores. And this is just the coalition's ministry, to say nothing of what the congregations do on their own. Do the congregations of CCLP minister to the people who live in their area? You be the judge: The 1980 population census revealed the area served by the CCLP congregations to be 43.5 percent white, 49.6 percent black, 7.5 percent Hispanic, 1 percent Asian. That same

year the membership figures of the CCLP churches showed a constituency of 43, 52, 4, and 1 percent in these same categories.

The negative forces that can hold a congregation back from fulfilling its ministry in this way are "a lack of vision in identifying the
needs of the community," said Pastor Steve Rode of San Antonio,
and ". . . an unwillingness to risk new ministries even though they
may not necessarily seem to have a direct return to the congregation." From deep in the heart of Texas his comments described the
challenge which Luther Place in Washington, D.C. met successfully.
As told in earlier chapters this congregation, located in the tough,
harsh neighborhood of Thomas Circle just north of the White
House, had to decide whether to get involved in its own neighborhood. It did, opening its doors as a place of hospitality and refuge,
a home for the homeless. Soon the row of buildings the church
owned on a nearby street were converted to service ministries to
meet the needs of those our society has thrown out or left behind,
abandoned on the streets not far from where those charged with
the stewardship of this nation sit in plush accommodations. With a
budget on voluntary contributions of now $1,400,000 a year, Luther
Place ministers each year to thousands of people who populate the
streets around it. This is one church which dared to identify the
needs of its community, and even more daringly to act in light of
those needs.

I could not help but be amazed at the many ways congregations
in this study carried out their ministry of caring for people. Christ
Lutheran Church in Roanoke has an outstanding track record in its
social ministry. Forty-six refugees to date have been sponsored. The
building is used monthly for programs directed at servicing the elderly, the mentally ill, and as space for local social service agencies.
Trinity Lutheran Church in Camp Hill developed its own debt-fore-
closure lending service to assist people in temporary need of assistance. Pastor Stephen Byrne was named 1986 Texas rural minister
of the year by a farming organization for his work in responding to
the needs of people afflicted by the farm crisis in his congregation's
community of Winters, Texas. MacArthur Park Church in San Antonio developed a program which provides daily food bags to the
needy. Epiphany Lutheran Church in Dale City, Virginia, was developed as a mission congregation by Robert Holley in the 1970s and
grew to include a pre-school and program for retarded children
among its ministries. And the list goes on. Not surprisingly, the
strong benevolent giving in many of these congregations extended
beyond their doors to embrace the concerns of the wider church.

There is no magic to quality care and outreach, just the doing of
it by both pastors and laity. If there is a "technique" which is the

key to all of this, it is the term popularized by Tom Peters: MBWA or "Managing By Wandering Around." He calls it the technology of leadership, ". . . the method by which leadership becomes effective in any well-run school, hospital, bank, single-store operation or industrial enterprise."[5] To which I would add the church, and revise the term to mean "*Ministry* by Wandering Around." It is exercised most importantly by pastors who are "in touch" with their people and their church's community. But its spirit really has to infect the entire congregation.

"MBWA? I didn't know there was such a thing," remarked a seminary professor when I mentioned the term to him. Indeed there is, and any pastor who is not doing it is probably not doing much of anything effective in his or her parish. The minimalist view which sees the exercise of the office of ministry—preaching the Word, administering the sacraments—as restricted only to what occurs at worship services has to be jettisoned. Cannot one be a bearer of the Word of God to people outside this setting? Does not every day provide the pastor who is "in touch" with that parish's community (what CCLP's Director, John Cochran, calls "being where your people are, when they are") opportunities for evangelism (speaking the Gospel), witness to Christ, service to others in his name, and inviting unbelievers to become part of the community of worship? And what shall we make of Jesus' itinerant wanderings? Or St. Paul's? Or St. Francis's? I submit that all effective ministry, including the formal exercise of the office of ministry in the worship service of the community which gathers around God's Word and Sacrament, is rooted in the practice of a pastor's "Ministry by Wandering Around."

How it is done varies from pastor to pastor. The key is to do it consistently and often. "I stayed out of my office as much as possible," remarked David Hunsberger of his years at St. John's Lutheran Church in Fairfield, Pennsylvania. "I simply tried to be available to the people, such as by eating regularly at the local breakfast shop, walking around the grocery store in our one-street town where I would meet quite a few of my members, etc." Pastor Bieber of Detroit talked of spending his Saturdays visiting the neighborhood bars in direct evangelism efforts. His laypeople accompany him on such visits to share in the work. Pastor Tim Ohlmann, who serves in an Hispanic neighborhood in Philadelphia, speaks Spanish and visits every home in the neighborhood every two years. In larger churches pastors resorted to small-group meetings to keep in touch with their people. At the huge Mt. Olivet Lutheran Church in Minneapolis, keeping in touch with 10,000 members translates into 88,000 cups of coffee a year—$4,000 in the annual budget—consumed at small-group meetings.[6] Pastor Dave Gleason recalled his ministry in rural East Berlin, Pennsylvania. Every morning he had coffee at the restaurant across the street from his church. He later estimated that 70 percent of the new members who joined the church during his pastorate were people he first met in those coffee-shop visits. When Peter Rudowski served a parish in Sharon, Ohio, he practiced his MBWA by spending regular afternoons in the local high school just "being available" to any student who wanted to stop by for a chat. He also spent considerable hours in the local meeting place in his town, the barber shop. In West Bloomfield, Michigan, Pastor John Freed is so well recognized (which takes considerable work, given the isolationist tendencies of suburbanites) that he was asked a few years ago to be the moderator in a public forum over the local school strike. John Cochran described his MBWA during his years at Emmanuel Lutheran Church this way:

> I was deliberately exposing myself to the neighborhood, making the conscious effort to be seen by people. So, when I went grocery shopping, I went to the Thriftway—not the Acme—and said hello to 'x' number of people as I pushed the cart around. The second important thing to do was to observe the protocol of the black community. For example, funerals. It is protocol in the black community, if you in any way know the deceased, even if he is not a member of your church, to go to the viewing and 'speak words.' Not to do so is considered arrogant and very inhospitable." [So it is also, I find, in farm communities.]

The net result of this, he went on to say, was to learn how to speak the Gospel in that culture. "I knew the tradition," he said, "but the people have to teach me how to say it and show me what works in their culture. The working out of faith and culture is not something I do in isolation, but what I and the people do together." Unfortunately, he said, most pastors are too arrogant to do this. They assume the people have nothing to teach them, that their pearls of wisdom are far superior to whatever the people have to offer.

In whatever way possible, these pastors were in touch with their members and their community. They spent nearly 70 percent of their time in direct involvement with their people and their community through preaching, teaching, leading worship, assisting committees, counseling, and the like. One-third of their visiting time, on average, was spent visiting non-members. They did Ministry by Wandering Around in whatever way they could in whatever situation it was needed. And they did it consistently.

Now, one would think that this should be obvious. Sadly, it is not. As I mentioned earlier, I made a practice having morning coffee or noon meals at the restaurant in the center of my one-intersection town. The response from people was unbelievable: "We never had a preacher do what you did before, at least not for the last twenty years. We did not quite know what to do with you, we were not used to it!" Why had no local pastor stopped by the corner restaurant to talk to people for the last twenty years? I don't know, yet it seems this oversight is the norm, not the exception. Pastor Neal Boese reported from his surveys and contacts with pastors that fully 70 percent of them do not call on members on a regular basis, let alone non-members. I have known pastors who not only do not live in the same town as their church, they do not even live in the same county!

This discussion has focused on the pastor's practice of "Ministry by Wandering Around," but it is not limited to the clergy. Laity have their fair share of work to do, too. The simple truth is that in most congregations 90 percent of all people who visit the church do so not because of the how beautiful the building looks, or the minister, or the zippy programs, or advertising.[7] They come because a friend or relative has invited them to come along.[8] So, evangelism begins with a Christian, any Christian, identifying people she knows who are not involved in church, and simply asking them, "Would you come with me this Sunday?" It is that basic. What forms, eventually, is a "spider web" of relationships which draw more and more people in and provide much more lasting stability to a congregation's membership than those who are brought in by and only known by the pastor. But how many laypersons overlook this most simple of opportunities, or take the time to find out?

Certainly the care and outreach ministries of the churches mentioned above were sustained and energized not by the pastor alone. Everyone was on board. The point is put well by Jurgen Moltman in *Hope for the Church*:

> The renewal of the church finally depends on what happens at the grass-roots level. And renewal at this level awaits, it seems to me, on the conscious reclaiming of the gifts of the Spirit on the part of the laity. These gifts, which in the New Testament are always identified as signs of the coming kingdom of God, are given to the whole people of God for ministry, for *diakonia*. . . .[9]

Ministry by Wandering Around (MBWA), it turns out, is not an activity restricted only to pastors. In lively congregations everyone gets into the act and does it as the means by which the parish seeks to make known the Gospel among its members, in its community, and in the world. Doing it is the engine which powers the congregation's commitment to quality care and outreach—which with quality worship and quality education are the ways congregations carry out their ministry of the Gospel and become a light to the world and to the church.

Challenge to the Church

The characteristics of excellence in parish ministry I have described in the preceding chapters are really nothing special. No one reading this book should be surprised that a sense of mission, pastoral leadership, lay commitment and ownership, and quality in worship, education, care, and outreach are the key components of congregational ministry. Indeed, every congregation does them all to some extent. The critical, strategic difference between the churches that stand out for what they do and those that wallow in mediocrity is nothing more or less than a commitment, a passion, an obsession with doing things well in a ministry.

This commitment to excellence is discernable in both pastors and laity. "Why is it," my intern pastor asked me, "that all other things being equal in a parish—people, location, etc. (and they generally are in the short run)—three pastors' performances are average at best, then a fourth comes in and really shines?" Some will say "luck," others a sudden outpouring of the Holy Spirit which enables the pastor and the people to grow in spite of themselves. But I think more often than not, the last pastor had a commitment to excellence in ministry which was head and shoulders above the rest. Or, in the case of laity, their image of themselves and commitment to excellence probably meant the difference between growth in ministry and stagnation over a series of pastorates.One of the pastors interviewed recalled his first parish, a "tough" congregation in the steel belt of Western Pennsylvania. For five years he struggled with them, calling parishioners to a higher vision of their church than they had. But, after he left, they proceeded to call a series of pastors whose self-image matched what he called their "collective inferiority complex." Now they have fallen from a single-call parish to being one church in a three-point call.

Why is it that some churches in an area—any area—decline, while others grow in ministry and, oftentimes, in numbers? Look again, and you will probably find a commitment on the part of the pastor and the people to quality in ministry which is a notch above other churches.

In short, the critical difference between healthy, growing congregations and other churches is not some secret formula for success. Their distinguishing feature is that they do the common, mundane, plain-vanilla boring tasks of ministry uncommonly well. They do so regardless of their size, socio-economic make-up, location, or environmental changes. They simply sought to do what Trinity, Camp Hill expresses in its mission statement: "We seek excellence in all our ministries."

It is just this commitment to excellence that the church needs if it is to grow in its ministry. That commitment is discernable in many corners of the church today. Careerism and the trappings of "professionalism" have eroded the "divine motive for ministry," the call, in the lives of many pastors. Laity have settled for mediocrity in ministry instead of expecting, encouraging, and supporting their pastors and each other in striving for competence and commitment. We have pursued survival and security over mission and service, in direct contradiction to Jesus' words of warning that those who seek to preserve their lives will lose them, but those who lose their lives for the sake of the Gospel's will find them. We have sought remedies for our problems in a host of paper programs produced by church staffers who have not been in the parish for years and who pull pastors and congregations in every conceivable direction with their favorite cause and separate agendas. Pastors and bishops alike busy themselves with doing everything but doing well the basic tasks of ministry: preaching, leading worship, teaching, and visitation.

In an Ash Wednesday sermon a few years ago I suggested that the one sin which we need to repent of most in the church is the sin of mediocrity, of settling for second best, of just "getting by" from year to year. We needed, instead, to commit ourselves to "what is excellent and worthy of praise" (Phil. 4:8) in doing the ministry of the Gospel. What would such a commitment to excellence entail? Let's start with the basics.

First, let's get straight on what the church is about in the world: getting the Gospel spoken through Word and Sacrament so that believers can be strengthened in their faith and witness and unbelievers brought to Christ. As simple as that sounds, it is not at all evident that we are in agreement on this. Ask people what the church exists for and you will get a variety of answers: The church as a social action agency, as a provider of programs, as the "sweet hour of prayer," as "the place my parents went to church," as a general dispenser of religious services. But a sense of what the church is basically to be about is lacking.

In a 1986 article in *The Lutheran* titled, "Lutheran Evangelism is a Joke," Rev. Neal Boese described with precision our current malaise:

> Our problem revolves around a confusion as to our purpose. Pastors and congregational leaders do not agree on our purpose, and from what I can determine, denominational leaders and seminary faculties do not agree on our purpose. We do not know what we are about or why we exist.[1]

Similarly, Carl Braaten writes in *The Apostolic Imperative:*

> Doing evangelism is the one thing that gives meaning to everything else the church must do. It is its *raison d'etre....* The root of Christian identity lies in its apostolicity. Apostolicity means doing the apostolic thing, namely, continuing the cause of Jesus under the conditions of its transformation through the events of Good Friday and Easter, as well as Pentecost and Ascension. There is no other way to retain continuity with the apostles than to keep on doing what they did—going with the Gospel, making disciples of all nations, baptizing them in the name of the Father and of the Son and of the Holy Spirit (Matt. 28:19). That is really all that mission is.[2]

In another article, "Evangelization in the Modern World," Braaten employs the criteria of Lutheranism's identity, its confessional principles, for evaluating our mission efforts so as to not lose sight of the church's basic purpose in the world and how it is carried out.[3].

The first of these, the principle of "grace alone," makes clear that the church's mission is revealed in God's unconditional love in Jesus. Thus, the church's mission is in truth God's mission, in which the church participates by grace. God, therefore, defines what the church is to be about.[4]

The principle of "faith alone" means that the church's missionary efforts cannot demand of those to whom it carries the Gospel any conditions of doctrine (orthodoxy) or behavior (orthopraxis) for their hearing of the Gospel. The principle of "Christ alone" centers all the church's efforts on the person of Jesus Christ as the only means of salvation. The principle of "Scripture alone" requires that all the church's mission efforts be critiqued by the authority of the Bible for the church's faith and life. The principle of what is sufficient *(satis est)* for the true unity of the church—the right preaching of the Gospel and the right administration of the Sacraments— serves to help the church clarify the ministry of the Gospel from cultural accretions and conditions in propagating the Gospel from one context or society to another.[5]

Last and perhaps most important, Braaten encourages the church to distinguish between the two ways God rules the world (the two kingdoms principle) so as to gain greater clarity in its mission efforts. That is, the church needs to distinguish (not separate!) its unique mission of proclaiming the Gospel from God's work through civil government and other secular institutions which work for world peace, justice, etc. The former task is the church's unique work in the world; the latter is something the church does in partnership—not separately or identified—with other God-appointed worldly agents.[6] Braaten suggests that some of our confusion in mission stems from lack of clarity regarding these two ways God works in the world:

> Have we perhaps been putting more time, attention, money, and people in the service of projects that fall to the left side of God's activity in the world, all doubtless good and necessary things in themselves? . . . These are integral to the church's total mission, but never as substitutes for the Good News which all persons need to hear under whatever circumstances they happen to be living.[7]

It is a matter of the church maintaining the proper distinction (please note: not separation, identification, or subordination!) between its unique work of preaching the Gospel which creates faith in Jesus and the good works which are the natural result of faith.[8]

Even a novice reading the Gospels can see that each one ends on the same note. The church is sent out into the world to follow the risen Lord Jesus and announce the Gospel of him to an unbelieving world so as to make new followers of Christ. And the Gospel itself is its own vindication for spreading it, for if Jesus' resurrection from the dead is the Good News that the church bears, then the message has an impact on the final outcome of every person's life—indeed, of the whole creation. News like that should not be withheld from anybody.

Second, let's get straight on where the church's work is most visibly and effectively done—in the parish. If the church is the community of Christians gathered to hear God's Word and share in the sacraments, then clearly the parish is the most visible, concrete manifestation of this. It is where "the rubber hits the road" and people are brought to Christ. Writes Jurgen Moltman:

> The local congregation is the future of the church. The renewal of the church finally depends on what happens at the grassroots level.[9]

Jacques Ellul's principle mentioned earlier, "Think globally—act locally," ought to be the motto that focuses and guides our planning and activity at all levels of the church. This means that the church must begin to commit a lot more time and attention—the marks of care—to the parish and what goes on there.

The National Church

In 1985 the Michigan Synod of the Lutheran Church in America called Rev. Neal Boese to take charge of a program of evangelism emphasis and growth (his story has been told earlier). He began his job not by sending out a mailing of all the great ideas and programs he or the evangelism committee had for pastors. Instead, he spent his first months visiting every pastor in the synod, listening to their concerns and discerning what was needed in evangelism emphasis. From that initial period were developed institutes on evangelism for pastors and laity which have been well-attended and respected.[10]

The experience of Center City Parish has also been mentioned in previous chapters. Besides its effects in congregations and among the pastors, it also produced a change in the relationship of parish pastors and staff people in the wider church. Commenting on this, John Cochran wrote in *Lutheran Forum Letter* how the relationship changed from one of natural adversaries (due to frustration, stupidity, insensitivity or simply the failure to communicate) to partners in ministry. He cited cases of staff people who were sensitive and teachable, willing to learn from the streets and from pastors and laity, who in turn became excellent teachers of parish ministry.[11]

Those two stories provide evidence of what the national church can do to care for the parish ministry. What contributes to such success is obvious: the willingness to listen to the needs and wisdom of those who are on the ground level of the church and shaping the activity of the wider church to allow those in the parish to do their work more effectively.

Unfortunately this approach is not always taken. Not a few in this study criticized the "program mentality" of denominational organizations today, characterizing many of them as "construed programs"

which "never come to fruition" anyway. One pastor characterized
them as ill-defined, ineffective, and of almost no help at all to the
local parish. "Most good pastors," he observed, "tend not to be
heavily involved in synodical programs."[12] Another simply said, "We
have found that synodical programs operate at a lower level of competence and expertise than we do in our parish." Added a layperson, "The problem with the wider church is that it always seems to
be reorganizing without getting anything done, and it is more concerned with paperwork than with people." Commented another, "I
have zilch reliance on the national church. It's best to stay away
from them, because they come at you with their own agendas for
parish ministry that are simply rationalizations which seek to justify
their own existence." Concluded another, "The national church
wants to write the agenda for ministry instead of listening to the
agenda of the people. Our social statements seldom touch the lives
of people in the pew."

I do not wish to engage in bureaucrat-bashing. The last comment points to the heart of the problem which exists between the
national church organization and the local church. Every organization tends to develop hierarchies in which, as one moves "up" in
the structure, one increasingly moves "away" from where the action
is and the product or service is being delivered. The same tendency
exists in the church. One layperson characterized the current state
of the national church as ". . . like government: It exists for its own
sake. The individual congregations exist to serve its needs instead of
the other direction." One pastor characterized it as a "franchise
mentality." Both point to what Barbara Hargrove, in her book *The
Emerging New Class,* describes as "the professionalization of the
church" in which the denominational churches have become modern bureaucracies. She writes:

> The typical denomination has a national structure that, regard-
> less of its official polity, is dominated by its full-time profes-
> sional staff. . . . The work of the church is handled by profes-
> sionals in much the same way that managers serve stockholders
> or staffs keep things going for legislators. Much of the work that
> is done in assemblies is in response to reports from these
> professional staffs and agencies. . . . Because of their own educa-
> tional background, they tend to create or commission educa-
> tional materials that reflect the staff's world view. . . . [They]
> attempt to require congregations to create local committee
> structures that reflect the structures of the denomination, so that
> there will be appropriate contact people to receive materials
> from each of the central boards and agencies. In other words, in

spite of much rhetoric about nourishing members, there are strong pressures to orient local congregations toward the central organization rather than towards local needs or interests. In general, the view of the church most natural to denominational staff is that of any large bureaucracy: the primary functions are found at the top of the hierarchy, and local staffs, like branch offices, provide services to clients in the pew.[13]

If the national church is to care—really care—for the local parish, then an entire reversal of this process must occur. The push has to be downward, not upward. The focus of what is most important to the church's mission must be what is happening in the local parish. The message that what is really important in the church's mission happens "off somewhere" beyond the local parish (which more often than not simply represents the agenda of whatever segment of the bureaucracy broadcasts its activity the loudest) must be squelched.

As a case in point, consider the way the advocacy movement, which has been a major drive in the Lutheran churches in recent years, has been conducted. An outgrowth of concerns raised in the 1960s to give the church a more visible presence in the political sphere, the advocacy movement has sought to create networks of Christians who will become involved in lobbying legislators to advance the legislative positions of the national church or local synods. Though these advocates may have been seeking to emulate the prophets of ancient Israel, the net result of their efforts has been less than prophetically inspirational. Where the prophets were publicly visible, the Lutheran advocacy efforts have largely been relegated to letter campaigns and backstage arguing with politicians by official church representatives. Where the prophets visibly proclaimed God's Word to the public social issues of their day, advocacy efforts have bogged down in back-room politicking on legislative minutiae to achieve results on which no unanimous agreement exists among believers. "Pastors and laypeople going about their neighborhoods soliciting signatures on petitions to support this or that piece of legislation is not what I understand the Bible to mean by evangelism," commented one pastor. Last, in focusing advocacy efforts on state, national and international issues, the advocacy movement has turned people's attention away from where the most visible, effective action could take place—the local community. Summarized one pastor, "Advocacy without proximity is hypocrisy. It is very easy and comfortable to write a letter to South Africa protesting apartheid. But what are you doing about the racism in your own community and church?"[14]

In calling for a more downward-emphasis, parish-focused denominational organization, the church would do well to draw on insights from secular organizations today, especially people like Tom Peters or John Naisbitt *(Reinventing the Corporation)*. Though the church is sometimes criticized for modeling itself along the lines of business corporations and trying to co-opt their management techniques, I believe that what some business people say about effectiveness in organizations should be heeded by the church. This is especially true when it comes to reversing the trend toward hierarchy in organizations—of which the church is one. In his pamphlet, "A World Turned Upside Down," Peters writes of the new shape of today's organizations. The old model was hierarchical, staff-centered, and several-layered, with complicated matrixes designed to coordinate activities. The new design is flat, front-line dominated, decentralized, and value-driven rather than tied to paper controls, with the focus on those actually delivering the service and a corresponding lean upper staff.[15] Unequivocally he states, "Most organizations are at minimum 600 to 700 percent overstaffed."[16] He cites as examples of the new, leaner, more responsive, more effective organization Nucor Steel, a $600 million dollar company which has a corporate staff, including secretaries, of twelve.[17] Also the Dana Corporation, which under Ren McPherson grew from $1 billion to $3 billion while reducing corporate staff from 600 to 150.[18] Or Bob Townsend, author of *Up the Organization,* who while at Avis had a personnel department of one.[19] The fallacy of the past was thinking that true genius in an organization resided in the upper echelons and in the executive suite. In truth, the best creativity and insight comes from people "on the firing line."

In light of these observations, it becomes crystal clear that the structures of many national churches today are organizational dinosaurs. Again, I will take the one I am most familiar with—the structure of the new Evangelical Lutheran Church in America. Its multi-layered scheme of congregations/synods/regional centers for mission/national organization with its divisions and commissions is a recipe for a bureaucratic goulash. The structure contains people who are out of touch with the local parish, yet churning out reams of paper and a plethora of programs to supposedly "meet the needs" of the pastors and people in the pew. It is a movement in exactly the opposite (and wrong) direction of the new organizational models which suggest fewer layers, leaner staff, and a focus on what is happening at the local level. The challenge to achieve excellence in the church in America in the years to come must begin with renewal "from below," or, in a less hierarchial-sounding phrase, "from the front lines." Indeed, in Latin and South America this is precisely where renewal in the church has taken place. In *The Continuing Frontier: Evangelism,* Mortimer Arias writes of ". . . the phenomenal movement of the Base Christian Communities, small grassroots communities of Christians which are renewing the Church and contributing to the renewal of society. There are more than 150,000 of these BCCs in Latin America. Some theologians are saying that these Christian communities of the poor—where scripture is read and dynamically related to their social context—are in fact a process of ecclesiogenesis, the reinvention of the Church from below: 'The church that is born from the people.' "[20]

Our context in America may be different, but I suggest that the principle at work in the Basic Christian Communities needs to take hold in our churches as well. Renewal begins at the grassroots, in the parish, where the people are. In practical terms, for the national church to focus on the parish means several things. First, as several pastors in this study suggested, invest the money where it will do the most good—in the parishes. One way is to support weaker churches, providing the financial stability for pastors to stay at smaller, less affluent congregations long enough to do effective ministry. Second, eliminate unnecessary layers, such as the regional offices in the new Lutheran denomination, for example. Why should the church need any more than three layers (congregations, synods, and national church)? Instead, foster creativity at the local congregation or in clusters of congregations in a small (i.e., less than county) area, such as the coalition ministries of Center City Lutheran Parish or Southeast Delaware District Lutheran Parish in the Southeast Pennsylvania Synod of the old Lutheran Church in America. Third, replace paper communications with person-to-person communications. Wipe out everything that smacks of elitism in the upper layers of the church's organization or fosters carreerism by suggesting to pastors that "life is better up here." Beyond this, the best approach might be the one suggested by a pastor interviewed: The church ought to buy Robert Townsend's *Up The Organization,* put it into practice and do a 180-degree turnaround.[21]

The Synodical Bishops

The one place in the church where a focus on the parish can begin in a most effective way is in the offices of the synodical bishops. What we need are parish-focused bishops who are not just interested in what goes on in their parishes, but who really care about the parishes they are called to oversee. The difference is where one puts one's time. Every bishop, I am sure, is very interested in what the parishes of his or her synod are doing, but caring demands more than being interested. It demands time, attention and focus. A simple law of human activity maintains that what you give your time and attention to is what you really care about. So it needs to become standard operating procedure that a bishop will visit every parish in his synod at least once a year. This has to be more than just a half-hour social call on the pastor or preaching at a service. It means spending time with the pastor, the pastor's family, and the church leaders and members to hear their concerns and in turn to communicate to them a vision of the wider ministry of the church. The latter alone, I dare suggest, would do more to promote better benevolence support than all the paper advertising produced by church staffers in a year.

Such meetings should have as their theme earnest dialogue between the bishop and the parish concerning the current state and future directions of the parish's ministry. At times this will mean calling slothful congregations and pastors to account and reminding them of what they are to be about as followers of the Lord. This may go against a certain view of Protestantism in which congregations and pastors view themselves as their own little synods and bishops. But the alternative of confessional unfaithfulness and driftwood ministries is far worse.

Bishops who choose to demonstrate real care toward their parishes may have to perform radical surgery on their calendars which are stuffed to the gills with meetings with commissions, committees, task forces, and the like. Said one pastor after he had seen a bishop's calendar, "How in the world can he do the ministry a bishop should do with a calendar like that?" Of course, the complaint will be that making such time is an idealistic, simplistic dream. I would respond that bishops who really care about the churches of their synod will make the time. It should not be too difficult in the new Lutheran denomination. Most synods contain fewer than 200 congregations. Finally, I am reminded of the story Tom Peters has told about Sam Walton, president of Wal-Mart stores. At 67 years young, he would spend a half-day a week in his office, a day and a half with his vendors and three days a week visiting his stores. He would visit all 700-plus of them at least once every year.[22] Why can't a bishop do the same with his congregations? Let the staff people go to all the conferences and committees. The bishop needs to be visible where the real Gospel mission takes place—the local congregation.

The bishop, like every pastor, needs to be a leader, not just an administrator greasing the wheels of the ecclesiastical machinery. Bishops can only develop a vision of what their synods can be if they really know what is going on in their synods and parishes, and can only do this by doing what every pastor needs to do—Ministry By Wandering Around. Visiting every congregation once a year, at the very least every other, in the way I have outlined would do much to enhance respect for the office of the bishop. Undoubtedly it would help foster better relations between the parish and the wider church. Perhaps, too, it would help cut down on the number of pastors who are permitted to bumble along in the parish from year to year, while the people suffer because no one is really holding them accountable to do their job and to do it well.

The Seminaries

Focusing on the local congregation begins in seminary where, supposedly, seminarians are trained to serve in parish ministry. I say "supposedly" because it cannot be said with certainty that this actually happens during those years of preparation. As Pastor Boese's earlier comments revealed, our seminaries are not all that clear about the mission of the church. Such lack of focus results in what a layperson called the "fragmented seminary curricula" which exposes seminarians to a wide-ranging diversity of theological subjects and disciplines without tying them into the one central theme— who a pastor is and what a pastor's purpose is in the parish.

"I came back from my internship with all sorts of questions about what goes on in a parish and what a pastor does," reminisced one pastor about his seminary training, "but all I got in my last year of seminary was another dose of Barth and Brunner. I was taught very little in how to actually 'run' a parish." My general observation is that seminaries are undecided about the real reason for their existence. They are split between being a training school for future parish pastors or a Master's program for those seeking to do future Ph.D work in theology. This dual orientation in turn manifests itself in the variety and types of courses offered in seminary curricula.

Especially needed are final-year courses and seminars which integrate theological training with actual parish situations. "Theologically, we are probably better trained than ever," said Pastor Greg Wenhold of Good Shepherd, King of Prussia, "but in terms of training for actual parish situations, there is very little being done in the seminaries." Laypersons mentioned lack of training in office administration, time management, and general management skills as serious failings of seminaries today. In particular, attention needs to be given in the final year to training soon-to-be-ordained pastors about the exercise of pastoral leadership in the critical first year of ministry in a new parish. We cannot take for granted that seminarians will pick up these skills on internship. We cannot assume that their supervisors will be skilled in such areas. In addition, unless a seminarian's first call is to be an assistant pastor in a large parish, newly-ordained pastors usually begin their ministry with a congregation much smaller than the one they served on internship—on average less than 100 worshippers on a Sunday. These congregations are often saddled with pressing financial problems, not unlike the one I went to in my first call, where I was greeted with the words, "I don't know why they send people right out of seminary to dying churches."

Future pastors need to be trained to function in small congregations, not the ones they experienced on internship. Since half of the Protestant congregations in America are less than 100 worshippers a Sunday, it behooves the church to prepare men and women to serve in these kinds of parishes, not hold before them the dream of a large congregation bursting with talent and programs. Many pastors will never serve in large churches, so training in pastoring the small-to-average size congregation is sorely needed.

A second major area seminaries need to emphasize is the actual doing of evangelism. Pastors, let alone laity, sorely need training in doing evangelism with unbelievers, baptized and unbaptized. This training is simply not offered in seminaries today. Seminarians receive no training in what to do in pastoral calling on members and non-members, in what traditionally was known as the "care of souls." To my knowledge, little is taught in the practice of personal evangelism outside of the pulpit or an organized effort of the congregation. Nor are theological discussions connected to the evangelization of the unchurched, reflecting again the dichotomy between what is taught in seminaries and the actual mission of the church. The point was acutely brought home to me in one continuing education course I attended. During a class session, I commented that what the professor was saying presented some interesting connections for dialogue with non-believers. His terse reply was, "Well, perhaps so, but I really can't say. In fact, if I was in a situation of having to talk about the faith to an unbeliever, I don't know what I would say. I'd probably shut up."

Third, seminaries need to discuss honestly and candidly what Richard John Neuhaus in *Freedom For Ministry* calls "The Pursuit of Holiness."[23] One's training in personal devotions and spiritual formation receives little attention in most seminaries. As a remedy one pastor suggested, "They ought to give everyone a copy of the daily office and teach them to read it." Another suggested building into the yearly curriculum a required week in a monastery. Seminaries should admit to the double standard that calls pastors to a higher standard of morality and personal conduct and discuss openly how one functions in light of that. Particular attention needs to be paid to a pastor's stewardship of money, use of time, the tension between following a call and planning a career and especially living with the double call to ministry and to marriage. The latter should not be reserved just for would-be pastors, but for their spouses as well. In fact, in its Senior pre-session at the start of the 1986-87 school year the Gettysburg Seminary designed just such a program for both pastors and their spouses. Finally, seminaries need to foster a collegiality among pastors and a real love for the parish ministry, instead of the subtle message sometimes transmitted to seminarians which says, "The parish is the enemy. They've really fouled things up out there and we are sending you out as our champions to fix it." This thinly-veiled contempt for the parish, accompanied by an elitist attitude which looks down on and questions the validity of the ministry of other pastors instead of appreciating them for the gifts they bring to the church must be rooted out. Pastor Robert Neumeyer's first priorities when Center City Lutheran Parish was established were to end competition and foster collegiality among the coalition pastors through common prayer, sermon study, and sharing of gifts and resources. The same has been done in many other settings, to the benefit of pastors and their congregations.

Simply put, we can no longer afford to act as though every parish is its own synod and each pastor his own bishop if the church is to be united in its mission of proclaiming the Gospel. Being centered on the parish does not mean isolationist parochialism. It means pastors and laity working together on the front line of the ministry of the Gospel, the parish. Such collegiality and teamwork begin in seminary in how one relates to one's fellow students and in how one regards the parish one is being trained to serve.

A final recommendation concerns the actual hiring of seminary faculty. If, as I have maintained in this book, the parish is *the place* where the church's ministry of the Gospel gets carried out in its most concrete form, and if, as I state above, the seminary's main function in the church is the preparation of people for the exercise of the office of ministry in the local congregation, then this needs to become the guiding principle in the hiring of seminary faculty. This is not always the case. In just my own ten years of ministry I have noted an increasing number of seminary faculty who have been hired with only minimal parish experience, often, it seems, out of a desire to appear "inclusive."

This is to say: Academic credentials, while necessary and not to be downgraded at all, should not be the only or main consideration. Nor should hiring be on the basis of quotas (sexual, racial, ethnic, or ecumenical). Rather, the key question, regardless of who is being considered, should be, "Does this candidate, by training, work history, and church activity, demonstrate a love and concern for the advancement of parish ministry?" Where this question is not raised consistently and seriously, seminary education is bound to steer into paths of mediocrity, subject to every trendy theological fad which comes down the pike, and increasingly distant from the practice of parish ministry.

The Local Congregation and Its Pastor

My last focus is on the parishes—the pastors and people who are where the rubber meets the road. Much of what needs to be done to revitalize parish ministry already has been mentioned in the previous chapters. This project has been dedicated to showing that really good ministry is being done in the church. Regardless of size, location or any other factor, pockets of excellence in ministry shine forth. We hear stories of turned-around congregations across the church; only a few are part of this study. Their example should be held up, applauded and taken as inspiration for what can happen any place, any time, where the ministry of the Gospel is carried out with a commitment to excellence. Led by Pastor Richard Neuhaus (1960-1977) and his assistant Pastor John Heinemeier (1967 on), St. John's the Evangelist Church in Brooklyn has been described as "a piece of work no one has come close to duplicating." Luther Place Church in Washington has a ministry to the homeless unparalleled in America, though its pastor, John Steinbruck, wonders why "what ought to be ordinary is looked on with amazement." Emmanuel Lutheran Church, Philadelphia, under John Cochran, was transformed from a dying, isolated white congregation to a thriving congregation totally immersed in neighborhood ministry. St. Paul's Lutheran Church in Lansdowne, Pennsylvania, was on its last legs just four years ago when Pastor Dee Littleton came. Today its attendance at worship services has doubled. The list goes on.

The point is this: no church has to die. No church has to or should be content with merely "hanging on" passively until Jesus comes. Any church in any location can grow numerically where there is a commitment to excellence in ministry. More important, even where numerical growth does not occur, the commitment to excellence in ministry can still make a church stand out like a shining light while others without a desire to excel are declining and falling by the wayside.

Such growth in ministry does not come easily. Noted Peter Rudowski, it requires ". . . a pastor who wants the church to grow, and is willing to put the time and energy into it to make it happen, and a membership willing to pay the very heavy price of growth." It requires investing the time and energy it takes to achieve quality in worship, education and outreach. It requires being willing to accept the conflicts which will arise as pastor and people struggle together to seek a faithful ministry of the Gospel. It requires resolving these conflicts openly and honestly, seeing them as an opportunity to teach the faith. It requires being open to the changes which any growth in ministry, let alone numbers, will bring to a congregation. Or, as Tom Peters remarked in a 1986 speech, "We've got to develop organizations which love change instead of hate it."[24]

So, the final issue is this: Getting started. In concrete terms, how do a pastor and laypeople go about getting started on the road to seeking excellence in all their ministries? In congregations which one pastor described as "burdened by a tradition of failure," how can tradition be reversed? The following is not a step-by-step "how-to" list, but may be good for starters:

For the pastor, who is the key catalyst in introducing a commitment to excellence in ministry in a parish, the commitment begins with his or her self-perception of being called by God to minister to the people of God in a particular place and time. He or she must determine to do that ministry until God through the church issues the call to serve in another community of the faithful in a new place. "Plan to stick around!" is the first step in planning for growth in ministry. Trust that God has called you to where you are *right now* and let this call guide you in your ministry. What Jerry Schmallenberger called "the divine call—motive for ministry" is the greatest source of strength to a minister. It frees a pastor from the "life is greener on the other side of the fence" syndrome, from careerism, from questioning the validity of one's ministry. It frees him or her to focus on the work at hand and leave other matters to God.

Second, focus on the basics of ministry, resolve to do them well and cut down (viciously) on all of the other distractions from the community, the wider church, and yourself which draw you away from your essential work of being a pastor to your congregation and community. Commit yourself to quality in every area of your activity. In looking back on Wallace Fisher's dynamic thirty-year ministry at Lutheran Church, Lancaster, his successors remarked:

People have remarked that Dr. Fisher was a genius intellectually and in his ministerial skills. But really his true genius was a gen-

ius of commitment. He was passionately committed to the ministry of the Gospel and had great expectations that when it was
proclaimed, people would respond.

As one pastor in this study suggested, seek constant evaluations
and feedback from your people on what you are doing and how
you can serve them better. Do this consistently, constantly, persist-
ently. Preach good sermons, not just in the sense of "putting on a
good show," but in terms of biblical and theological content that
addresses real-life issues (remember Luther's counsel to preach a
true grace which forgives real, not fictitious sins[25]). Lead worship in
an exciting manner that dramatizes what the liturgy is about. Teach
well. Care for your people in whatever ways are needed. Don't get
bogged down reading the mail, filling out forms, etc. Adopt the advice of Pastors Bob Holley and Stephen Youngdahl: "Touch a piece
of paper only once." Don't become a "tinkerer" in details which are
an excuse for not doing what a pastor is basically called to do.
Don't let laity slough off on you matters like the care of the property, the finances, secretarial work and altar care which are their responsibility. (By the same token, laypeople, don't let your pastor get
away with taking over work you should be doing either). Don't "go
off" to do ministry elsewhere. Stick close to home: your church,
your community, your county.

Several years ago Joseph Sittler wrote an essay entitled "The Mac-
eration of the Minister" which addresses now as it did then the critical importance of focus in the ministry:

> It is, I think, not true that the parish demands of its minister to
> become simply an executive officer of multiple activities. The
> congregation is likely to accept, support and be deepeningly
> molded by the understanding of Office and calling which is pro-
> jected by its minister's actual behavior. It will come to assess as
> central what the pastor, in the actual performance of ministry
> and use of time, makes central.[26]

Third, practice "Ministry by Wandering Around." Get out of your
office and get in touch with your people and your community.
Spend most of your time in the personal delivery of pastoral services (preaching, leading worship, teaching, pastoral care, etc.). I
suggest as a guideline a general rule proposed by Tom Peters: "Any
person . . . spending less than 70 percent of his time out of his office is essentially fouling up."[27]

Fourth, promote mission, not "bodies and bucks." "Avoid today's
obsession with statistics. Critical ministry is the thing," commented
John Steinbruck. Work at developing a vision of what God is calling

the congregation to do in their community, their neighborhood. Let the numbers take care of themselves.

Fifth, constantly seek new ways to improve what you and the congregation do in your ministry of the Gospel. Avoid the "same old same old" routine. Anything can probably be done better or different next time. While long-term planning is helpful in embodying a vision of ministry for the congregation, effective planning and goal-setting focuses on the next day, the next week, the next month.

Sixth, take action! Seek out opportunities which can dramatize for people the mission and goals of the congregation. Do things which will cause people to sit up, take notice, and climb on board the congregation's mission. The idea is to reverse the congregation's negative self-image and tradition of failure by introducing the perception that such good things are happening in the congregation that people will want to be a part of it. And this cannot start too soon! To quote Peters again, "The question is, 'What are you going to do in the next fifteen minutes. . . .' The new manager [read "pastor"] who hasn't taken action on two or three issues of critical importance by the end of his first morning on the job is falling behind."[28]

This leads to the seventh and final suggestion, which is enlisting the support of members for the congregation's ministry. Though these steps are directed primarily at pastors, in truth they can be undertaken by laypersons at any place in their congregation's organization. It is best described by Peters as the "small-win" approach, which is: Look first to achieve small successes which can become the building blocks to larger ones in the future. In every organization exists some corner in which a small win can take place. Start there and build on them. Along with this, identify and nurture what Peters calls "champions"—people who are excited about the organization and want to see it grow. Almost every organization has them. Leave the areas where nothing can be done and the recalcitrant people for a later day. Concentrate on achieving a few small wins to build momentum and nurture people who want to see growth.[29] And don't forget to thank such people for their efforts. (My intern pastor was fond of saying, "Recognition is the breakfast of champions.")

Once the process has begun, build on it by developing commitment among the members throughout the congregation. To build on the early successes, use a "participative planning model" which gets members into a thinking and planning process where their creative talents are put to use. Pastors in this study accomplished this in varying ways, but the principle was the same. A practice of Peter Rudowski's has been to break the Council down into small groups that meet once a year to discuss and dream about their congregation's future ministry. From such meetings came reports of great ideas which were then farmed out to committees for further work and implementation. Rudowski has applied the same principle to the "annual drudgery" of the Annual Congregational Meeting. All in attendence are assigned to small groups in which they suggest ideas for their congregation's growth which are then referred to the Council. Bob Holley devotes a section of church Council meetings to what he calls, "Pulse of the Parish." In it every person at the meeting is invited to say anything—an idea, a praise or criticism, etc.—about anything in the parish. It naturally leads to new ideas and programs. Another church, Immanuel in Pflugerville, Texas, used a long-range planning committee or "think-tank" to develop ideas for the congregation's ministry. The pastor's role in all of this is to guide from the biblical and churchly tradition. Occasions such as these provide excellent opportunities for teaching the faith as both pastor and laity work together towards a faithful ministry. And they promote lay ownership and commitment—which is the machine which transforms small-wins into big-wins. With the pastor and the people united in their commitment, who knows on what new adventures of faith God will lead a parish.[30]

Will Pursuing Excellence in Ministry "Work"?

"Will this work? Will doing all this make my congregation grow?" is, I am sure, a question many will ask. My answer? I don't know. The Spirit works faith, when and where he pleases, in those who hear the Gospel (John 3:8). The main thing is to get the Gospel said as best we can. That means having a commitment of excellence. Where pastors and congregations seek to do this, growth usually occurs, but there is no guarantee. Sometimes, despite the best efforts of pastors and laypeople, there is no response. But, since it is the Spirit who works faith, it is not up to us anyway. What is up to us is faithfulness to the tasks of ministry our Lord has given us. Faithful witness to the Gospel, not statistical figures, is the final standard of success for a Christian, a congregation, or the church (see Luke 17:10; Matthew 7:21-23; Philippians 2:12-16; 1 Timothy 6:11ff; 2 Timothy 4:1-8).

To be sure, the picture of excellence in ministry I have sketched here conflicts at points with another major viewpoint regarding renewal and growth in congregations—the Church Growth Movement. By statistical standards, its teachings and methods have proven themselves successful in numbers of churches in all sorts of settings. Its proponents and their followers have helped refocus attention in the church on the nature of Christianity as a missionary enterprise and forced people on all sides to strive for greater clarity in understanding this mission. In insisting upon seeing that proclamation of the Gospel is inseparable from the context in which it is proclaimed, the Church Growth Movement has underscored the vital relationship of faith and culture. And the movement has provided congregations with pragmatic, practical actions to take to increase its membership. In its methods and approaches, the Church Growth Movement is perhaps without equal.

Despite its obvious numerical successes, however, questions must be raised about the Church Growth Movement, especially in light of the description of excellence in ministry presented in these pages. I do not with to delve into a full-scale critique of the movement; numerous books and articles have done just that. Still, since this section began with the pragmatic issue—"Will this work?"—some comments on the Church Growth Movement are appropriate here.

First, there is no simple equation relating excellence in ministry with numerical growth in a congregation. As the name suggests, the Church Growth Movement is interested in just that: church growth, getting people to be committed to Christ and become responsible members of a church.[31] True evangelism is not primarily the proclamation of Gospel, but persuading people to follow Christ and join the church.[32] The emphasis is on the results. The church's mission (for which Matthew 28:18-20 becomes the central scripture) is to gather converts and multiply congregations.[33] Indeed, faithful witness to the Gospel comes to mean effectiveness in getting a church to grow: "All theories of church growth which have not produced results should be cast aside in the desire to be faithful to God."[34]

It is certainly not my intention to dampen enthusiasm for growth in any church. Certainly the New Testament and church history reaffirms that Christians who carry out the Great Commission of Matthew 28 should expect to see converts to the faith. But the equation of church growth with faithfulness to the church's mission is too simplistic and focuses attention away from what excellence in ministry is all about—faithful witness to the Gospel. Interestingly enough, none of the pastors and congregations which were a part of this study defined their focus in ministry as seeking to grow numerically. Again and again their emphasis was on being faithful witnesses to the Gospel, faithful bearers of Christ in the world. For example, Pastors Lehman and Hoover of Trinity Lutheran Church, Lancaster, had this to say about the issue of church growth in their congregation:

We have not focused on numerical growth. We are focused on being faithful to the Gospel and to pastoral work. Whatever happens as a result of that happens.

Luther Place Church, Washington, described its ministry along the same lines:

By evangelism we mean to exemplify (not impose) the presence of God, and as such it is our intention to be a light amidst the darkness of our nation's capital. . . . In this context Luther Place has turned the corner and is experiencing congregational growth. However, that is not our goal. We are to be faithful, not numerous! And it is by "our fruits" that we must be known—not by the statistical critieria so important to denominational corporations and to the evangelistic hustlers of electric media.[35]

Similar comments were made by pastor after pastor about their church and its ministry, all of them focusing on the primary concern of being faithful to the ministry of the Gospel to which Christ calls his church.

Thus, the concern to be raised of the Church Growth Movement can be phrased in the words of Pastor Richard Bieber in the chapter on mission: "Too many churches are not focused on Jesus." For all its concern to carry out the Great Commission of Jesus, the question has to be raised as to whether the Church Growth Movement is focused on the person of Jesus as he is revealed in the Scriptures and comes to his church through the Word and Sacraments.

It is not at all clear that the Church Growth Movement is concerned that the Christ people are being asked to follow is the Christ of the Bible, that the Gospel being propagated for people is the true and pure Gospel, or some other (see Galatians 1:8). When one reads, for example, C. Peter Wagner's *Your Church Can Grow* and finds such diverse expressions of the Christian faith as Robert Schuller's Crystal Cathedral, Jerry Falwell's Thomas Road Baptist Church, and James Kennedy's Coral Ridge Presbyterian in Fort Lauderdale being lauded as growing, successful churches, one has to conclude that the question of confessional identity and faithful witness is not the critical issue for the Church Growth Movement. Successful practical efforts in gaining new members is.

Nor is it surprising that this would be the case, for in truth the Church Growth Movement is not founded on theology, but sociology. In effect, it takes Matthew 28:18-20 as the center of scripture and the starting point for theology. From that point it draws upon sociological insights and organizational dynamics and uses them as the vehicle for doing the church's mission. So, for example, the "Homogeneous Unit Principle," a key means for evangelism in Church Growth Movement teaching, becomes irrefutable as a description of the way human beings like to behave in relating to others, but is questionable as a means for describing God's mission in the world in Christ and how that affects what the church is and does.[36] Again, Peter Wagner's "Seven Signs of a Growing Church" are in truth descriptions, couched in religious language, of what is essential for any organization to grow: leadership, members organized for growth, sufficient services in the organization to meet the needs and expectations of its membership, a healthy balance in the group life of the organization between large, moderate, and small-group activities, membership that is homogeneous, the use of recruitment methods that work, and strong organizational identity and priorities.[37] With very slight modifications, the principles and methods of the Church Growth Movement could be used just as effectively to achieve growth in a Boy Scout troop, volunteer fire company, business corporations in general, or any other organization.

This is not to say such insights are not helpful to the church. But, they are no substitute for, nor should they take precedence over, faithful witness to what the Lord calls the church to be and do in the world. Wrote Wallace Fisher:

> Alert parish pastors will resist the how-to-do-it books which suggest that parish renewal can be had by some special approach or method—Bible study groups, a downtown counseling center, a coffee house, a lay academy, Bible preaching, a sound educational program, an evangelism program, a jazz liturgy, et. al. These are tactics for parish renewal and ongoing witness. Any one or all of them can be useful. That depends on the situation and the cultural climate. But there is only one strategy: the objective-subjective proclamation of God's Word of judgment and grace must make it clear that God speaks relevantly to the human condition. . . . The primary need is for clergy, lay leaders, and the general membership to come under the Word of the Lord in judgment and grace so that the Holy Spirit can call, persuade, and enlighten persons who, in their freedom, respond.[38]

In sum, the Church Growth Movement offers some excellent insights into the way organizations grow. The very presence of the movement forces the church to examine its life more closely and define its mission more precisely. But the "bottom line" of excellence in ministry is never a matter simply of increased membership—which, for all its attempts to prove otherwise, is still the dominant agenda for the Church Growth Movement. The measure of the church's effectiveness in fulfilling Christ's missionary command can never be something as crass as "Will it work?" For in the preaching of the Gospel God will work through the Holy Spirit to work faith. The real results, then, are up to the Lord.

Actually, one of the best insights on excellence in ministry and church growth comes from an unexpected source, and is a fitting conclusion. It is an adaptation of a passage from the book *Further Up the Organization,* by the former Chief Executive Officer of Avis Rent-a-Car, Robert Townsend:

> Growth is a by-product of the pursuit of excellence and not itself a worthy goal.
>
> Please pursue excellence—not growth. If it leads to flat spots in your sales and profit curves [Christians, read "membership growth and offering reports"], so be it. Who says human beings or human organizations don't need breathing spells?
>
> If everyone in your company [church] and all your customers [your community] know your goal is excellence, then you have done your job. Keep on doing it, and take what comes. Let everybody enjoy being part of the best even if it's not the biggest.
>
> Chateau Haut-Brion didn't get to where it is trying to become Coca-Cola.[39]

Exactly. Parishes do not need to die. Nor do they need to just "hang on" for dear life until the Lord returns. The Lord himself promises that the power of death will not prevail against his church (Matt. 16:17). In other words, Jesus settles the question of survival. This leaves the church free to focus on the one thing necessary: its ministry of the Gospel. And though the church's mission is to all the corners of the earth, the bottom line is not net growth in numbers. It is faithfulness to the Gospel's mission in the world. Being faithful means pursing excellence in all dimensions of parish ministry by all members in the parish. Pursuing excellence in parish ministry, as the examples in this book have shown, can be done by any parish under any circumstances.

Churches, Pastors, and Laypersons of this Study

Pastors

Richard Bieber — Pastor, Messiah Lutheran Church, Detroit, Michigan

Neal Boese — Former pastor at three churches in Texas and at First St. Paul's Lutheran Church in Hastings, Nebraska. Recently served as the Director of Evangelism Emphasis for the former Michigan Synod of the Lutheran Church in America. Now serving a parish in Lexington, Kentucky.

Steve Byrne — Senior Pastor of St. John's Lutheran Church in Winters, Texas.

John Cochran — Former pastor of Emmanuel Lutheran Church, Philadelphia. From 1978 through 1987, Director of Center City Lutheran Parish, a coalition ministry between inner-city Philadelphia parishes.

Terry Daly — Pastor of Cana Lutheran Church in Berkley, Michigan.

David Deal — Pastor of Trinity Lutheran Church in Yeadon, Pennsylvania.

William Derrick — Senior Pastor of Salem Lutheran Church, Brenham, Texas.

Richard Dowhower — Senior Pastor of Trinity Lutheran Church, Camp Hill, Pennsylvania.

Wallace Fisher	Pastor Emeritus of Trinity Lutheran Church, Lancaster, Pennsylvania.
John Freed	Pastor of Holy Spirit Lutheran Church, West Bloomfield, Michigan.
David Gleason	Former pastor at Trinity Lutheran, East Berlin, Pennsylvania. Now serving at Palm Lutheran Church, Palmyra, Pennsylvania.
Myron Herzberg	Pastor of St. Paul's Lutheran Church in Remsen, Iowa.
Jack Hoffman	Associate Pastor, Trinity Lutheran Church, Lancaster, Pennsylvania.
Robert Holley	Formerly Mission developer/pastor of Epiphany Lutheran Church in Dale City, Virginia. Now pastor of St. Mark's Lutheran Church in Charlottesville, Virginia.
John Holmer	Formerly assistant pastor at Good Shepherd Lutheran Church, Cincinnati and now pastor of Hope Lutheran Church in Midland, Texas.
David Hunsberger	Former pastor at St. John's Lutheran Church, Fairfield, Pennsylvania. Now serving at Trinity Lutheran Church in New Holland, Pennsylvania.
Scott Ickert	Pastor of Holy Trinity Lutheran Church, Leesburg, Virginia.
Larry Lehman	Senior Pastor, Trinity Lutheran Church, Lancaster, Pennsylvania.
Dolores Littleton	Pastor of St. Paul's Lutheran Church in Lansdowne, Pennsylvania.
Richard Michel	Formerly mission developer/pastor at Holy Cross Lutheran church in Teays Valley, West Virginia. Now serving as pastor of Trinity Lutheran Church in Ephrata, Pennsylvania.
D. Lee Muehlbrad	Senior pastor of Immanuel Lutheran Church, Pflugerville, Texas.

Richard John Neuhaus	Former pastor at St. John's the Evangelist Lutheran Church in Brooklyn, New York City. Now Director of the Rockford Institute Center on Religion and Society in New York City. Editor of "Religion and Society Report" and "Lutheran Forum Letter". Author of *The Naked Public Square, Freedom for Ministry,* and other books.
Tim Ohlmann	Pastor of St. Simeon's Lutheran Church in Philadelphia.
Greg Pile	Pastor of New Centerville Joint Parish, New Centerville, Pennsylvania.
Mark Radecke	Pastor of Christ Lutheran Church in Roanoke, Virginia.
A. Stephen Rode	Senior Pastor of Christ Lutheran Church, San Antonio, Texas.
Peter Rudowski	Senior Pastor of Good Shepherd Lutheran Church, Cincinnati, Ohio.
Edward B. Saling	From 1977 through 1987, Director of Southeast Delaware District Lutheran Parish, a coalition ministry among parishes in southeast Delaware County, Pennsylvania.
Jerry Schmalenberger	Senior Pastor of St. John's Lutheran Church, Des Moines, Iowa, and the author of several books of sermon collections.
George Schwanenberg	Pastor of MacArthur Park Lutheran Church in San Antonio, Texas.
John Siefken	Pastor of Prince of Glory Lutheran Church in Madison Heights, Michigan.
Larry Smoose	Pastor of God's Love Lutheran Church in Newtown, Pennsylvania.
John Steinbruck	Senior Pastor of Luther Place Lutheran Church in Washington, D.C.
William Waxenberg	Senior Pastor of Living Word Lutheran Church in Grapevine, Texas.
Greg Wenhold	Pastor of the Lutheran Church of the Good Shepherd, King of Prussia, Pennsylvania.

Stephen Youngdahl — Senior Pastor of Shepherd of the Hills Lutheran Church, Austin, Texas.

Laypersons

Dr. Robert Benne — Professor of Religion at Roanoke College, Roanoke, Virginia. Author of the *The Ethic of Democratic Capitalism,* et al.

David Houck — Member of St. James Lutheran Church, Wenksville, Pa., one of three churches in the Bendersville Lutheran Parish I currently serve. A lifelong participant in synodical activities, he currently serves on the Synodical Church Council of the Lower Susquehanna Synod of the E.L.C.A.

Carol Jarvis — David Houck's daughter and former member of St. James Lutheran Church, Wenksville. Now a member of God's Love Lutheran Church in Newtown, Pennsylvania.

Pat Smith — Coordinator of Volunteer Ministry at God's Love Lutheran Church in Newtown, Pennsylvania.

Lael Cordes-Pitts — Member of Hope Lutheran, Midland, Texas. Served as a lay professional in Messiah Lutheran, Panama City, Florida, and in several church social agencies.

Two questionnaires were returned without names being given by laypersons of St. John's Lutheran Church in Des Moines, Iowa, and Good Shepherd Lutheran Church in Cincinnati, Ohio.

The Churches of the Study

Most of the congregations included in the research were studied with their presently serving pastor. In some cases, however, the congregation's ministry under a former pastor was selected; where this is the case, the pastor's name is followed by an asterisk (*). As I mention in this book the parishes I have served, I include information on them as well.

The figure "CCC" stands for "Confirmed/Communing/Contributing Membership." Lutheran churches designate people who are confirmed and who contribute or commune at least once a year to measure the active membership of a congregation.

Most of the congregations in the study are congregations of the former Lutheran Church in America, which merged January 1, 1988 with the American Lutheran Church (ALC) and the Association of Evangelical Lutheran Churches to form the Evangelical Lutheran Church in America. Where an ALC or LCMS (Lutheran Church—Missouri Synod) church was contacted, the notation is listed in parenthesis following the church's name.

Iowa

St. John's Lutheran Church, Des Moines
Rev. Jerry Schmalenberger, Senior Pastor

St. John's is located in downtown Des Moines. Founded in 1865, its reputation has been built on a history of strong preachers (of which Pastor Schmalenberger is the latest). The membership is now 3500 baptized, 2500 CCC.

St. Paul's Lutheran Church, Remsen
Rev. Myron Herzberg, Pastor

Remsen is a typical rural small-town in the northwest corner of Iowa, not far from Sioux City. A farming community, it has suffered from the farm-belt crisis of the last few years and is also witnessing an influx of new residents from the Sioux City area.

Pastor Herzberg came to St. Paul's after graduation from the Lutheran Seminary at Gettysburg in 1980. Since then attendance has grown from 85 to 120 worshippers per Sunday, with 285 baptized members.

Michigan

Cana Lutheran Church, Berkley
Rev. Terry Daly, Pastor

Cana Lutheran Church was created in 1980 out of a merger of two Detroit congregations and an already-existing Lutheran church at the current site of Cana. The town is an established suburb of Detroit. Pastor Daly came to the congregation in 1984.

Messiah Lutheran Church, Detroit
  Rev. Richard Bieber, Pastor

  Located in inner-city Detroit, but away from the renovated
  downtown area, Messiah was founded in 1897. When Pastor Bieber arrived there in 1958, the congregation had declined mark-
  edly as its original constituency migrated to the suburbs.
    The area is now a mix of blacks, Hispanics, Asians, Arabs,
  and white migrants from Appalachia. So, now, is the church,
  with an attendance around 350 a Sunday. A truly phenomenal
  mark of this church is that out of a budget of $210,902 the
  church gives away a whopping 45 percent to outside causes
  (most Lutheran congregations do not even approach half that
  much). Of that figure, 96 percent goes to other-than-synodical
  benevolence ministries.[1]

Prince of Glory Lutheran Church, Madison Heights
  Rev. John Siefken, Pastor

  Madison Heights is a middle-class suburb twelve miles northwest of Detroit. The church, averaging close to 200 a Sunday in
  attendance, is located just a quarter-mile west of I-75 and has
  been gaining 15 adult members a year in spite of the surrounding decline in the area's population. Since Pastor Siefken came
  in 1969 the church has doubled in size. The story of Prince of
  Glory and Pastor Siefken's ministry there is told in greater
  length in the chapter on mission.

Holy Spirit Lutheran Church, West Bloomfield
  Rev. John Freed, Pastor

  Located in one of the more affluent suburbs of Detroit, Holy
  Spirit was a struggling mission congregation when Pastor Freed
  came in 1969. The church now has over 500 baptized members
  with an average worship attendance close to 200. One of its
  unique ministries is its Saturday evening worship service.

New York City

St. John's the Evangelist Lutheran church (LCMS)
  (*) Richard John Neuhaus, Senior Pastor (1961-1977)
  (*) Rev. John Heinemeier, Assistant Pastor (came in 1967)

  St. John's was originally a German immigrant parish founded in
  1854 in the Williamsburg section of Brooklyn, located between
  the areas of Bedford-Stuyvesant and Greenpoint. During the

1940s and 50s the church declined dramatically in members due to urban migration. When Neuhaus arrived in 1961 the rolls listed 70 communicant members. Within the first year of Neuhaus' ministry and thereafter the church experienced dramatic increases in membership and worship attendence as it served a predominantly black, but increasingly Hispanic, neighborhood. The strengths of the congregation were its programs of worship, education, and social ministry.

Ohio

Good Shepherd Lutheran Church, Cincinnati
Rev. Peter Rudowski, Pastor

Good Shepherd was founded in the early 1950's. It is located just off I-71 in the middle- to upper-middle class suburbs northeast of Cincinnati. The church had hit a low point in its history at the time of Pastor Rudowski's arrival in 1974. Since then it has grown sizeably in members, program, and in building, adding two expansions within a ten-year period.

I served Good Shepherd as an intern pastor in 1976-77.

Pennsylvania

Emmanuel Lutheran Church, Philadelphia
(*)Rev. John Cochran, Pastor (1967-1978)

Emmanuel Lutheran began in 1966 as a German Lutheran congregation, but like many inner-city churches, the congregation experienced tremendous decline during the 1940s and 50s as its neighborhood changed. In the early 1960s the Southwark Plaza Housing Project was built in the four blocks surrounding the church. The church had become a typical inner-city declining White church in a now largely black neighborhood.

Pastor Cochran arrived in 1967. The membership then consisted of 170 members, eight of whom were black, with an average attendance of 55 a Sunday. In the next eleven years, Emmanuel became a 1000-member, mostly black (though German-speaking services still were held) church and added a school to its program of ministry.

St. Simeon's Lutheran Church, Philadelphia
Rev. Tim Ohlmann, Pastor

St. Simeon's, in the Hunting Park section of North Philadelphia, is another inner-city congregation which went through a decline during the middle of this century as its original German constit-

uency moved out of the neighborhood. The church's community
is now largely black and Hispanic, with some white and Asian
groups as well. All of these groups are now represented in the
congregation, which averages in the low 80s in attendance.

God's Love Lutheran Church, Newtown
Pastor Larry Smoose
Mrs. Pat Smith, Coordinator of Volunteer Ministry

God's Love was referred to me by several people because it is
the only congregation which is growing in its area (a part of
Bucks County north of Philadelphia just now becoming increasingly suburbanized). Founded in 1971, the church experienced
only minimal growth until Pastor Smoose's arrival in 1976. Since
then the parish has grown from 50 at Sunday worship to nearly
225.

St. Paul's Lutheran Church, Lansdowne
Rev. Dolores Littleton, Pastor

Lansdowne is an old, largely working-class community just outside of West Philadelphia. The church declined during the 60s
and 70s from 800 to 200 members. Pastor Littleton came in 1983
to a congregation that was in a "make-or-break" situation. In
four years the attendance has doubled, from 50 to 100 people,
new services have been added, and major building renovations
made.

Trinity Lutheran Church, Yeadon
Rev. David Deal, Pastor

Yeadon is a border community to West Philadelphia and has
been undergoing racial transition for some time. Since Pastor
Deal came to this congregation in 1984, it has integrated and attendance has risen from 55 to the low 80s.

St. Mark's Temple Lutheran Church, Clifton Heights
(*)Rev. Daniel Biles, Pastor (1978-1985)

Clifton Heights is a strongly ethnic Roman Catholic lower mid-
dle-income suburb of West Philadelphia. The church, located in
a row-home neighborhood, began as a mission in 1952 with the
name St. Mark's Lutheran. In 1959 the church merged with Temple Lutheran Church, a declining West Philadelphia congregation
whose members had moved out to the suburbs.

The merger created an instant church of 250 people a Sunday, but by my arrival in 1978 the parish had declined back to its pre-merger size of about 100 a Sunday. From 1978 through 1985 it maintained a stable congregation of 90 to 100 worshippers a Sunday and added a Nursery School, a second Sunday service (with weekly Communion), a fuller liturgical calendar, and increased educational opportunities.

Lutheran Church of the Good Shepherd, King of Prussia
Rev. Greg Wenhold, Pastor

Good Shepherd founded in a then-rapidly growing, transient, bedroom-community near Valley Forge in 1957. By the mid-1970s the church peaked at 250 worshippers a Sunday, then witnessed a decline to 125 during the early 1980s. Pastor Wenhold began his pastorate in the mid-1980s and, within two years, the parish rebounded to its former size. In the very fertile mission field that is King of Prussia, its potential for ministry is awesome.

Trinity Lutheran Church, Camp Hill
Rev. Richard Dowhower, Senior Pastor

With over 2,700 members, Trinity is the largest Protestant congregation in Central Pennsylvania. Camp Hill is a suburb of Harrisburg, Pennsylvania's state capital, from whose working force the church draws many of its members.

Trinity Lutheran Church, Lancaster
Rev. Larry Lehman, Rev. Jack Hoffman,
Rev. Penrose Hoover, Pastors
Rev. Dr. Wallace Fisher, Pastor Emeritus

Trinity is located in the heart of Lancaster. The story of the congregation has been well-documented in many books by Pastor Fisher, most notably *From Tradition to Mission*.

Trinity Lutheran Church, East Berlin
(*)Rev. David Gleason, Pastor (1972-1981)

East Berlin is a rural community twenty miles northeast of Gettysburg, Pennsylvania. The church experienced strong growth and liturgical renewal during Pastor Gleason's work there in the 1970s and early 1980s.

St. John's Lutheran Church, Fairfield
    (*)Rev. David Hunsberger, Pastor (1975-1985)

Fairfield is a rural community fifteen miles southwest of Gettysburg. St. John's was the result of a merger in 1970 between a
Lutheran and a Reformed church in the town. Pastor Hunsberger's ministry there saw the formation of a strong Lutheran identity in the parish and increased worship life.
    I served the church as a first-year Field Education student
from the Gettysburg Seminary.

Bendersville Lutheran Parish, Bendersville
    Rev. Daniel Biles, Pastor

This is a three-point parish in the orchard country of Upper Ad-
ams County. I began my ministry there in January of 1986. The
three churches—St. James in Wenksville; Christ, Aspers; Bethle-
hem, Bendersville—respectively average 49, 62, and 108 worshippers a Sunday.

Palm Lutheran Church, Palmyra
    Rev. David Gleason, Pastor

The congregation was organized in this suburb of the famous
chocolate-town of Hershey in 1745. Its average Sunday attendance is around 350. Pastor Gleason began his ministry there in
1985.

New Centerville Lutheran Parish, New Centerville
    Rev. Greg Pile, Pastor

Pastor Pile came to this joint parish in 1975 upon seminary graduation. Together the parishes now average over 250 worshippers
a Sunday. The parish is located in a rural area just south of the
Somerset exit of the Pennsylvania turnpike, about 70 miles
southeast of Pittsburgh.

Texas

Hope Lutheran Church, Midland
    Rev. Jon Holmer, Pastor

Midland is a large town in West Texas which was caught in the
oil depression of that area during the mid-1980s. The parish was
organized in 1962 and hit a peak attendance in 1969 of 105 a
Sunday. Pastor Holmer came to the church in 1984 from Good

Shepherd Church in Cincinnati. In spite of the effects of the community's economic troubles, the parish has grown again. Its 1985 attendance of 80 per Sunday was a fifteen-year high.

Immanuel Lutheran Church, Pflugerville (ALC)
Rev. D. Lee Muehlbrad, Senior Pastor

The small town of Pflugerville is located just north of Austin off I-75. The area is undergoing a transition from its rural roots due to suburbanization from the expansion around Austin.

St. John's Lutheran Church, Winters (ALC)
Rev. Stephen Byrne, Senior Pastor

The church was established in 1904 in this farming and ranching community. Pastor Byrne came to the parish in 1984. During his years there the parish has taken a leadership role in ministry to those hit by the farm crisis.

Salem Lutheran Church, Brenham (ALC)
Rev. William Derrick, Senior Pastor

Brenham is a rural town of 9,000 people, situated between Austin and Houston. The church, an older congregation founded in 1854, has seen 120 members join in the last eight years.

Christ Lutheran Church, San Antonio (ALC)
Rev. A. Stephen Rode, Senior Pastor

Pastor Rode came to this congregation in 1976.

These ALC congregations were referred to me through the bishop's office of the Southern District—ALC.

Mac Arthur Park Lutheran Church, San Antonio
Rev. George Schwanenberg, Pastor

Mac Arthur Park serves two major constituencies in its area: the military community (there are seven military basis in San Antonio) and the Hispanic native residents. From both communities it gains many members of non-Lutheran background. Pastor Schwanenberg came as pastor/developer in 1960. The church now averages 610 worshippers a Sunday and has a paid staff of 65.

Living Word Lutheran Church, Grapevine
  Rev. William Waxenberg, Senior Pastor

  Grapevine is a suburb nestled between Dallas and Fort Worth.
  Pastor Waxenberg came as pastor/developer to the area and
  founded the church in 1980. The church draws strongly from
  people of non-Lutheran background and is now over 400 baptized members.

Shepherd of the Hills Lutheran Church, Austin
  Rev. Stephen Youngdahl, Senior Pastor

  Pastor Youngdahl was called as pastor/developer in 1976; the
  church was organized in 1977. Located in an upper-middle- to
  upper-income suburb of Austin, the church has added a second
  staff pastor (in 1984) and has now 228 families. Twenty-five percent of its members come from non-Lutheran backgrounds.

Virginia

Christ Lutheran Church, Roanoke
  Rev. Mark Radecke, Pastor

  The parish is a church of 780 members located in suburban
  Roanoke. The church has a strong social ministry outreach
  through its own programs and groups which use its building.

Epiphany Lutheran Church, Dale City
  (*)Rev. Robert Holley, Pastor (1975-1985)

  Pastor Holley came to Dale City in 1975 as a pastor/developer.
  Located in a growing suburb of transient population south of the
  nation's capital, it grew to 220 average worship on Sunday.

St. Mark's Lutheran Church, Charlottesville
  Rev. Robert Holley, Pastor

  Pastor Holley came to this church, located just off the campus of
  the University of Virginia, in 1985.

Trinity Lutheran Church, Leesburg
  Rev. Scott Ickert, Pastor

  Leesburg is located in northern Virginia, within commuting dis-
  tance of the nation's capital. Trinity is located in a middle-class
  section of the town.

West Virginia

Holy Cross Lutheran Church, Taeys Valley
  (*)Rev. Richard Michel, Pastor (1982-1984)

> Taeys Valley is an upper middle-class, transient, suburban community of people from largely Baptist and Roman Catholic backgrounds. In his two years there the church grew from scratch to 115 members.

Washington, DC

Luther Place Memorial Church
  Rev. John Steinbruck, Senior Pastor

> The church is located just a few blocks north of the White House in an area known for its drugs, prostitution, and street people. Like Messiah Lutheran Church in Detroit, Luther Place is one of those amazing churches which manages to give away to outside causes almost as much money as it spends on itself. In 1985 it spent $230,000 on current expenses, $216,330 on non-synodical benevolence.[2]

The source to Notes (1) and (2) is the 1987 Yearbook of the Lutheran Church in America.

All Scripture quotations are from the Holy Bible: Revised Standard Version (Division of Christian Education, National Council of the Churches of Christ, 1971).

Quotations and citations from the Augsburg Confession are from the *Book of Concord,* Theodore Tappert, ed., (Phila: Fortress Press, 1959).

Preface

1. Winthrop Hudson, *Religion in America* (New York: C. Scribner's Sons, Inc., 1973), p. 441. See also "Whatever Happened to the Lutherans?" in *Forum Letter,* Richard Neuhaus, ed. (Vol. 16: No. 1), April 25, 1987.

Chapter I

1. David Gleason, "All This Lutheran Stuff About Word and Sacraments Really Works," *Dialog* (Vol. 18: No. 2), Spring, 1979, p. 88.

2. Eric Gritsch and Robert Jenson, *Lutheranism* (Philadelphia: Fortress Press, 1976), pp. 5-6.

3. *Augsburg Confession,* Article VII.

4. *Lutheran Identity* (Strasbourg: Institute for Ecumenical Research, 1977), pp. 16-28. With thanks to Rev. Dr. Eric Gritsch for suggesting and supplying this reference to me.

5. Warren Bennis and Bert Nanus, *Leaders* (New York: Harper and Row, 1985), pp. 190-203.

6. *Rite Site* (Vol. 4: No. 2), July, 1986. Published by the Central Pennsylvania Synod, Lutheran Church in America.

Chapter II

1. Wesley Fuerst, "On Biblical Perspectives Of Mission," *The Continuing Frontier: Evangelism* (New York: Division for World Mission and Ecumenism, Lutheran Church in America, 1984), p. 21.

2. John Cochran, "Urban Ministry: A Time For Learning," Forum Letter, Richard Neuhaus, ed. (Vol. 14: No. 5), June 1, 1985. For another classic history of what a renewed understanding of mission can do for a church, see Wallace Fisher, *From Tradition To Mission* (New York: Abingdon Press, 1965).

3. Carl Braaten, *The Flaming Center* (Philadelphia: Fortress Press, 1977), p. 12.

4. Richard John Neuhaus, *Freedom for Ministry* (New York: Harper and Row, 1979), p. 105.

Chapter III

1. Neuhaus, *Freedom for Ministry,* p. 177.

2. Bennis and Nanus, *Op. Cit.,* pp. 26-67.

3. *Ibid.,* pp. 2-3.

4. Part V, "Leadership," Chapter 16, "Attention, Symbols, Drama, Vision —and Love" in Peters and Austin, *A Passion For Excellence* offers some excellent reading on the details of effective leadership, especially the sections on "Things To Do Now."

5. Pastors might be interested in evaluating their exercise of leadership by using the "Leader/Non-Leader" chart in Peters and Austin, *A Passion for Excellence,* pp. 418-421.

6. *Ibid.,* p. 92.

7. Tom Peters and Nancy Austin, *Op. Cit.,* p. 312.

8. Bennis and Nanus, *Op. Cit.,* pp. 44-45.

9. *Forum Letter,* Richard Neuhaus, ed. (Vol. 15: No. 11), February 13, 1987, pp. 6-7.

10. Jerry Schmalenberger, "The Divine Call: Motive For Ministry, *The Lutheran* (Vol. 24: No. 11), June 4, 1986, p. 32.

11. Augsburg Confession, Article V.

12. For further good reading, see Mark Chapman, "Ordination as Rite and Responsibility" in Lutheran Forum (Vol. 21: No. 1), Lent, 1987, pp. 18-23 and Robert Jenson, *Visible Words* (Philadelphia: Fortress Press, 1978), pp. 188-203.

13. Lyle Schaller, *Growing Plans* (Nashville: Abingdon Press, 1983), pp. 47-48. See also Neuhaus, *Freedom for Ministry*, pp. 54-60.

14. Neuhaus, *Freedom for Ministry*, pp. 212-213.

15. Theodore White, *A Breach of Faith* (New York: Dell Publishing Co., 1975, pp. 407-432.

Chapter IV

1. Tom Peters, *Think Small—It's A Bold Idea* (Palo Alto, California: Excel/, 1986), p. 5.

2. Dietrich Bonhoeffer, *Life Together* (New York: Harper and Row, 1954), p. 55.

3. *Ibid.*, p. 86. See also Howard Stone, *The Caring Church* (New York: Harper and Row, 1983).

4. By focusing on the exercise of the priesthood of all believers among the members of a church for each other I do not mean to imply that this is all that there is to the concept. In truth it extends to the Christian's witness within the structures of life in society.

5. In fact, this unoffical greeter's work often goes so unnoticed by the other members that, when such a person moves, dies, or leaves the congregation for some other reason, he or she is not replaced by someone else, and a valuable service in the congregation is lost.

6. Bonhoeffer, *Op. Cit.*, pp. 90-109.

7. Further comments on the work of lay leaders at Trinity can be found in Wallace Fisher's *From Tradition to Mission*, especially pp. 169ff.

8. Peters and Austin, *Op. Cit.*, p. 273.

Chapter V

1. Dietrich Bonhoeffer, *Letters and Papers from Prison* (New York: Macmillan Publishing Co., 1973), p. 416.

2. Gleason, *Op. Cit.*, p. 90.

3. Leigh Jordahl, "The Cup Has Its Problems," *Lutheran Forum* (Vol. 21: No. 1), Lent, 1987, p. 6.

4. Jacques Ellul, *Perspectives on Our Age* (New York: Seabury Press, 1981), p. 27.

5. Peters and Austin, *Op. Cit.,* p. 10.

6. *Lutherans In Step* (Vol. 17: No. 2), July-August, 1986.

7. I have heard, however, of one anonymous survey which discovered that the factor most often cited by people as the reason they returned to a church after their initial visit was the cleanliness of the women's washroom.

8. The exceptions to this general rule seem to be congregations which are blessed with a high-visibility location, the "cathedral" church downtown which relies heavily on its reputation through newspaper, radio, TV, and Yellow Page advertising, and churches which serve a general region than a specific neighborhood or community.

9. Jurgen Moltmann, *Hope for the Church* (Nashville: Abingdon Press, 1979), pp. 21, 34.

Chapter VI

1. Neal Boese, "Lutheran Evangelism is a Joke," *The Lutheran* (Vol. 24: No. 15), September 17, 1986, p. 40.

2. Carl Braaten, *The Apostolic Imperative* (Minneapolis: Augsburg Publishing House, 1985), p. 11, 55.

3. Carl Braaten, "Evangelization in the Modern World," *The Continuing Frontier: Evangelism* (New York: Division for World Mission and Ecumenism, Lutheran Church in America, 1984), p. 39.

4. *Ibid.*, pp. 38-39.

5. *Ibid.*, p. 39.

6. *Ibid.*

7. *Ibid.*, p. 40.

8. See *Braaten, The Flaming Center,* Chapter 3, "The Identity and Mission of the Church" for additional discussion of this topic, especially the section, "Norming the Mission by the Gospel."

9. Moltmann, *Op. Cit.,* p. 21.

10. For further information, see *The Lutheran* (Vol. 25: No. 11), May 20, 1985, "Making Outreach No. 1"

11. See John Cochran, "Urban Ministry: A Time For Learning" and Harvey Peters, "The Parish As Place" (New York: Division for Mission in North America, 1986).

12. I would put the stress here on pastors not being *heavily* involved in synodical and national church affairs. All good pastors will, as a part of their proper exercise of the ministry of the Gospel, devote some time to the service of the wider church, but without losing sight of where their priority in ministerial service lies. Trouble begins where outside involvements become an escape from the parish's needs or are sought as the basis for validity in ministry.

13. Barbara Hargrove, *The Emerging New Class* (New York: The Pilgrim Press, 1986), pp. 122-124.

14. Parker Palmer in /cf21/The Company of Strangers (New York: Crossroad Publishing Company, 1981), pp. 143ff, offers an interesting discussion on the ineffectiveness of "conventional politics and backstage bargaining" vs. the effectiveness of public actions for achieving change in society—citing the decline from the sixties to the seventies in progress towards equal rights and justice as a case in point.

15. Tom Peters, *A World Turned Upside Down* (Palo Alto, California, 1986), p. 16.

16. Tom Peters and Robert Townsend, *Excellence in the Organization* (Chicago: Nightingale-Conant Corp., 1986), Tape 1.

17. Peters and Austin, *Op. Cit.*, p. 376.

18. *Ibid.*, p. 375.

19. Peters and Townsend, *Op. Cit.,* Tape 4. By contrast, when the new Evangelical Lutheran Church in America first advertised in November of 1986 for executive positions in its national headquarters, the Personnel Department listed fifteen job openings, not including secretaries.

20. Mortimer Arias, "Evangelism and the Poor and Oppressed," *The Continuing Frontier: Evangelism* (New York: Division for World Mission and Ecumenism, Lutheran Church in America, 1984), p. 55.

21. Robert Townsend, *Further Up the Organization* (New York: Alfred Knopf, 1984). See, for example, pp. 106, 172-178. Peters and Austin, *Op. Cit.,* pp. 373-378 also has some interesting ideas on "de-

bureaucratizing." For "de-bureaucratizing" in an ecclesiastical context, see L. David Brown, "Decentralizing For Mission," *Forum Letter* (Vol. 14: N14), May 1, 1985, pp. 7-8.

22. Peters and Austin, *Op. Cit..*, p. 375.

23. Neuhaus, *Freedom for Ministry,* pp. 185ff.

24. Tom Peters, "How Your Organization Can Achieve Excellence," Speech delivered to the Greater Baltimore Committee, Baltimore, Maryland, October

23, 1986.

25. Gritsch and Jenson, *Op. Cit.,* p. 139.

26. Joseph A. Sittler, *Grace Notes and Other Fragments* (Philadelphia: Fortress Press, 1981), p. 65.

27. Peters, "An Evening With Tom Peters."

28. Peters and Townsend, *Op. Cit.,* Tape 1. See also an excellent discussion of making the most of the first year in a new parish by Lyle Schaller in *Activating the Passive Church* (Nashville: Abingdon Press, 1981), pp. 136-146.

29. Tom Peters, *The Excellence Challenge* Audiotape (Palo Alto, California: Excel/Media, Inc., 1985), Side 2.

30. Lyle Schaller, *Growing Plans* (Nashville: Abingdon Press, 1983) offers some helpful suggestions as to tactics one might use in developing a congregation—as long as it is remembered that tactics for growth are just that: Tactics, not the Gospel itself.

31. Peter Wagner, *Your Church Can Grow* (Glendale, Cal.: G/L Publications, 1976), p. 12.

32. *Ibid.,* p. 141.

33. Arthur Glasser, "An Introduction to the Church Growth Perspectives of Donald Anderson MacGavran," in *Theological Perspectives on Church Growth,* Harvie Conn, ed. (Nutley, N.J.: Presbyterian and Reformed Publishing Co., 1976), p. 26.

34. *Ibid.,* p. 22.

35. John Steinbruck, "Luther Place Memorial Church: A Church as Refuge/Sanctuary," *Cities,* Fall, 1983, p.8.

36. The Homogeneous Unit Principle (HUP) is most succinctly described by its originator, Donald MacGavran, as the observation

that, "People like to become Christians without crossing racial, linguistic, or class barriers" (Wagner, *Your Church Can Grow*, p. 110). Which is, of course, exactly the way any human, Christian or not, prefers to join any group, the church or not. It is a sociological principle, not a theological one. It overlooks the fundamental nature of the church as a community created by Christ in which human divisions are no longer barriers between people, that as such the church, manifested in each local congregation, is a proleptic community whose life together anticipates and foreshadows in the present the universal oneness of all the nations of the world in the future God prepares for his creation.

The HUP is most vigorously defended in Peter Wagner's book, *Our Kind of People* (Atlanta: John Knox Press, 1979). I find his attempts to prove a biblical basis for the HUP unconvincing and methodologically unsound; Scripture is used in a "proof-text" method to support a pre-determined position rather than examined on its own grounds.

37. Wagner, *Your Church Can Grow*, p. 159.

38. Wallace Fisher, *Preface to Parish Renewal* (Nashville: Abingdon Press, 1968), pp. 31-32.

39. Townsend, *Further Up the Organization*, p. 86.

The Alban Institute:
an invitation to membership

The Alban Institute, begun in 1979, believes that the congregation is essential to the task of equipping the people of God to minister in the church and the world. A multi-denominational membership organization, the Institute provides on-site training, educational programs, consulting, research, and publishing for hundreds of churches across the country.

The Alban Institute invites you to be a member of this partnership of laity, clergy, and executives—a partnership that brings together people who are raising important questions about congregational life and people who are trying new solutions, making new discoveries, finding a new way of getting clear about the task of ministry. The Institute exists to provide you with the kinds of information and resources you need to support your ministries.

Join us now and enjoy these benefits:

CONGREGATIONS, The Alban Journal, a highly respected journal published six times a year, to keep you up to date on current issues and trends.

Inside Information, Alban's quarterly newsletter, keeps you informed about research and other happenings around Alban. Available to members only.

Publications Discounts:

- ☐ 15% for Individual, Retired Clergy, and Seminarian Members
- ☐ 25% for Congregational Members
- ☐ 40% for Judicatory and Seminary Executive Members

Discounts on Training and Education Events

Write our Membership Department at the address below or call us at (202) 244-7320 for more information about how to join The Alban Institute's growing membership, particularly about Congregational Membership in which 12 designated persons receive all benefits of membership.

The Alban Institute, Inc.
4125 Nebraska Avenue, NW
Washington, DC 20016